The GOSPEL of JOHN

The Gospel of John
A Beginner's Guide to the Way, the Truth, and the Life

The Gospel of John
978-1-7910-2792-6
978-1-7910-2795-7 *eBook*

The Gospel of John: DVD
978-1-7910-2794-0

The Gospel of John: Leader Guide
978-1-7910-2793-3
978-1-7910-2796-4 *eBook*

Also by Amy-Jill Levine

Entering the Passion of Jesus:
A Beginner's Guide to Holy Week

Light of the World:
A Beginner's Guide to Advent

Sermon on the Mount:
A Beginner's Guide to the Kingdom of Heaven

The Difficult Words of Jesus:
A Beginner's Guide to His Most Perplexing Teachings

The Gospel of Mark:
A Beginner's Guide to the Good News

Witness at the Cross:
A Beginner's Guide to Holy Friday

Signs and Wonders:
A Beginner's Guide to the Miracles of Jesus

AMY-JILL LEVINE

A BEGINNER'S GUIDE TO THE WAY, THE TRUTH, AND THE LIFE

The GOSPEL of JOHN

Abingdon Press | Nashville

The Gospel of John
A Beginner's Guide to the Way, the Truth, and the Life

Library of Congress Control Number: 2024937327
978-1-7910-2792-6

MANUFACTURED IN THE UNITED STATES OF AMERICA

Walter Gabriel Mayo
April 7, 2015–October 21, 2023

May his memory be for a blessing.

CONTENTS

Introduction ix

Chapter 1. The Wedding at Cana (John 2) 1

Chapter 2. Nicodemus and the Samaritan Woman 23
   at the Well (John 3 & 4)

Chapter 3. The Healing of the Man at the Pool (John 5) 47

Chapter 4. The Man Born Blind (John 9) 63

Chapter 5. Foot Washing (John 12 & 13) 79

Chapter 6. Mary Magdalene and Doubting Thomas 107
   (John 20)

Epilogue: Breakfast with Jesus 133

INTRODUCTION

In the Beginning

With its own version of the big bang, the Gospel of John announces itself with "In the beginning was the Word." For John, the beautiful world that God so loved, the world brought into creation with complete order, the world described in Genesis 1 as "very good," has become more beautiful, more ordered, and even better. The fourteen-verse Prologue to the Gospel—a theological treatise, an echo of biblical Wisdom, and a poem—not only speaks of the Word but it also announces itself via words. More, it tells us that the very words we use, words that shape how we understand the world, will now have different, even transcendent meanings.

"In the beginning"—in Greek *en archē*—echoes the Greek translation of the Hebrew Bible. John sends us to the beginning of creation and says, "Listen again." This time, now that you know the story of Jesus, you will hear creation differently. You should be able to see his presence, and that of the Spirit, on every page. Such retrospective reading was how the followers of Jesus in the early centuries of Christianity read their Scriptures. John helps with this re-visioning by telling stories of Jesus that replay many of those ancient texts: turning water into wine evokes Isaiah's vision of the great messianic banquet (John 2), Jesus compares himself to a magical serpent that saved people from death (John 3), he meets a woman at a well and the conversation turns to marriage (John 4), and so on.

For Genesis, the beginning is aural not visual: in the beginning was the word (Greek: *logos*, as in biology, words about life, or Decalogue, the "ten words," what have come to be called the "ten commandments"). Ancient Israel was an aural rather than visual culture. It heard its stories rather than pictured them; the Scriptures were chanted rather than illustrated in a book or a carving. People heard the words, over and over again; they were cultural memories, hardwired into their consciousness.

When Jews at the time of Jesus chanted Psalm 33:6, "By the word of the Lord the heavens were made, and by the breath of his mouth all their host," they would have recalled creation. More, they would have known the rest of the psalm and brought those verses into their understanding of creation, for God "loves righteousness and judgment; the steadfast love of the Lord fills the earth" (Psalm 33:5). To say, "God so loved the world" (John 3:16) is to hear the psalm. To see Jesus submit to crucifixion and not respond to violence with violence, their minds may have turned to Psalm 33:16-17, "Not is a king saved by a great army; a warrior is not delivered by great strength. The [war]horse is a false hope for salvation, and by its great strength it cannot escape." The rest of the psalm tracks with the Gospel, so the psalm interprets creation and creation interprets the psalm, and we readers add our third and fourth interpretations to the chorus.

The biblical stories in what the church came to call the Old Testament repeat with variations on a theme: rival brothers and sisters, infertile women and the birth of children, exile and return. John will repeat many of these themes, but in a new key. What is old becomes new, and what is new takes on richer meaning because of what came before.

When ancient prophets encountered the divine, the Bible explains, "The word of the Lord came to" them (e.g., 1 Kings 19:9, where this word came to Elijah). The word is so mysterious, so transcendent, that its presence is sensed in what seems to be its absence. First Kings 19 continues by noting that on Mount Horeb (another name for Mount Sinai) Elijah experienced first a great wind, and then an earthquake, and then fire, but then after the fire "a still small voice" (KJV) or "a sound of sheer silence" (NRSVue; 1 Kings 19:12). "When Elijah heard it...": Heard what? The silence? Then "a voice came to him" and asked, "What are you doing here?" John asks the same thing of those who hear the Gospel's voice: What are you doing here? What brought you to this place? What good news do you need to hear? What challenge are you called to face?"

The Greek of Genesis 1 sets a clear start time: "In the beginning, God made the heaven and the earth." Prior to the start time, there is nothing. The original Hebrew, however, begins with a temporal clause, "When God began to create the heavens and the earth" or "When, in the beginning, God created the heavens and the earth...." The focus is on a process: something was already present, and God changes it. The change is not from nothing to something. Rather, in the Hebrew, the change is from disorder to order, for "When in the beginning God created the heavens and the earth," the earth was what the Hebrew describes with the rhyming words *tohu vavohu*, "without form, and void" (KJV) or "complete chaos" (NRSVue).

John speaks of hearing consistently, for in the Gospel one person hears the word, and then brings another into the fold. "The wind—the spirit—blows where it wants, and you hear the voice of it," says John 3:8; Jesus states, "My sheep hear my voice. And I know them, and they follow me" (John 10:27). The Johannine Jesus states that even the dead will hear his voice. In the beginning was the word—the spoken voice. How could we not listen?

When we read John's Gospel "in the light" (yes, we're getting to the light) of the original Hebrew, we see anew what God does: God tames the chaos, just as God stills the storms. Nothing is simply that, nothing: it is neither good nor bad; it is just empty. Chaos is far worse, which means that divine creation is even better than we might have considered. Indeed, the Hebrew for create, *bara*, as in "God created the heavens and the earth," is a term predicated only of God.

When John says, "In the beginning," the scripturally aware listener will hear Genesis 1, and think of the creation, as only God can create, of order from chaos. The scripturally aware listener will also know that God creates by speaking order into existence. And when

John continues, "in the beginning the Word was with God, and the word was God," Aramaic-speaking Jews will do more: they will nod, because they will be in full agreement. To understand why, we need to know how Jews spoke (another verbal notice) about the divine.

The Word

In the third chapter of the Book of Exodus, Moses encounters a burning bush, which turns out to be a manifestation of God. During their conversation, Moses explains to God that he needs more information to fulfill his commission of telling Pharaoh, the Egyptian ruler, to free the Israelites he has enslaved.

"Look, I come to the children of Israel," asks Moses, and "I say to them, 'The God of your ancestors sent me to you,' and they say to me, 'What is his name?' what shall I say to them?" (Exodus 3:13). The next verse reads, as translated from the Hebrew, "And God said to Moses, 'I will be what I will be,' and he said thus, 'You will say to the children of Israel, "I will be" has sent me to you.' And God also said to Moses, 'Thus you will say to the children of Israel, YHWH, the God of your ancestors, the God of Abraham, the God of Isaac, and the God of Jacob, has sent me to you. This is my name forever, and this is my memory from generation to generation" (Exodus 3:14-15).

The divine name consists of four Hebrew letters: *Yod* (comparable to the Greek *iota*, the smallest of the consonants), *heh*, *waw* (Hebrew-speakers today pronounce the letter *vav*), *heh*, hence the English YHWH. We do not know how the letters were pronounced, since ancient Hebrew lacks marks that function as vowels. "Yahweh" is a good guess, but it remains a guess. Problems continue in that the initial identification, in Exodus 3:12, is not YHWH, but *ehyeh asher ehyeh*, "I will be what I will be." *Ehyeh* is the first-person singular of the verb meaning "to be." The letters *yhwh*—you can see the *y* and the two *h*'s in *ehyeh*—form the third-person singular, "he will be" or "he is" or even "he causes to be." It would have been easier had God said, "My name is Bob."

The name YHWH is ineffable, which means it cannot be pronounced. Not only can it not be pronounced in that we do not know how it was pronounced, according to Jewish tradition it is too sacred to be pronounced. Leviticus 22:32 forbids profaning the divine name. Therefore, Jews use circumlocutions when we find the name in biblical readings or in prayers. The letters may spell out YHWH, but the synagogue congregation reads "Adonai," which is Hebrew for "my lord" or "my sovereign."

By the time of Jesus, additional circumlocutions were gaining in popularity, including in translations. First-century Jews in Galilee (where Nazareth and Capernaum are) and Judea (home to Bethlehem and Jerusalem) spoke Aramaic, a language very much like Hebrew (as Spanish is like Portuguese, or Dutch is like German). Aramaic-speaking Jews referred to the deity as *memra*, which means—wait for it!—the WORD. Why? Because God creates by the word. Thus, when John writes, "in the beginning was the WORD," Aramaic-speaking Jews would agree.

"And the word was with God," absolutely, for with a word God created the heavens and the earth. "And the word was God," absolutely, since *memra*, the circumlocution for YHWH, means Word. For Jews, and for John, the divine is encountered not in the picture but in the story, not in the visual but in the hearing.

Jesus will tell doubting Thomas, "Because you have seen me, you have believed. Blessed are those who have not seen and believe" (John 20:29). They believe not because of what they have witnessed, but because of what they have heard. The last line of the Gospel, John 21:25, reinforces the importance of the word: "There are many other things that Jesus did; which, if every one of them were written, I suppose that the world (Greek: *kosmos*, as in "cosmic") could not hold the books that would be written." The books would be, in antiquity, read aloud.

Like any good poem, John's opening verse suggests multiple ideas, each tumbling upon the next. Along with the *memra*, the Aramaic

Word, John's comment about being "with God in the beginning" would have reminded listeners of Wisdom (Hebrew: *hochmah*; Greek: *sophia*). According to Proverbs 8:1-36, Wisdom, personified as a woman, "calls," "raises her voice," exhorts the people to "hear," since as she says, "All the words of my mouth are righteous." More, Wisdom is, like the Word, present at creation: "The Lord [YHWH] created me as (or at) the beginning of his way . . . at the first, before the beginning of the earth . . . I was beside him, like a little child (or master worker)." The *Logos* in John 1, with God in creation, is thus another form of *Wisdom*, but he is more than Wisdom, since he is not only *with* God, but *is* God.

This distinction is elided in the Wisdom of Solomon, where neither word nor wisdom is something created; rather, they are both a part of the divine. This Jewish book, written in Greek and contained in the Catholic and Eastern Orthodox canons, proclaims, "God of my ancestors and lord of mercy, who made all things by your word, and by your wisdom have prepared humanity" (Wisdom 9:1-2a). In Wisdom 9:9-10, the writer insists, "with you [God] is wisdom; she who knows your works and was present when you made the world. . . . Send her forth from the holy heavens, and from the throne of your glory send her," which is what God does by sending Jesus to earth. Wisdom 9:17 asks, "who has come to know your counsel, unless you have given wisdom, and sent your holy spirit from on high?" In retrospect, Christian readers here will encounter the Trinity.

Finally, the Greek term *logos*, John's term, would have resonated with people schooled in Greek philosophy. John is no slouch when it comes to writing for an educated audience. The Stoics used the term *logos* to describe the order of the world. Philo, the Jewish philosopher from Alexandria, Egypt, and a contemporary of Jesus, even speaks of the word, *Logos* (Philo writes in Greek) as the *archangelos* ("chief messenger," or "archangel") who stands on the border between the Creator and what is created and so functions as an intermediary between divinity and humanity (see Philo's *Who Is the Heir of Divine Things?*).

According to Genesis 1:2, in the chaos, at the beginning, "darkness covered the face of the deep, and a *ruach elohim* (Mighty wind? Divine spirit? Both?) hovered/swept/brooded over the face of the waters." The Hebrew term *ruach* can be translated "wind," "breath," or "spirit." The Hebrew word *elohim* is usually translated "God"; it appears in Genesis 1:1 with this meaning.

However, *elohim* can also function as an adjective, as indicating "mighty as God is mighty" or in the old English expression, "God-awful," which means "full of awe as in the presence of the divine." Since the context is ocean chaos, "mighty wind"—like a hurricane or typhoon— makes sense. But the term can also mean "the spirit of God," and that is how the Greek translation understands the verse. Whether we hear a reference to a gale-force wind or to the spirit of God will depend on how we understand John's language. As we'll soon hear, "the spirit blows where it will" (John 3:8).

Light of the World

God begins to order creation by speaking Light into existence: "Be light!" (Genesis 1:3). The common translation "let there be light" doesn't get the big bang effect. Nor does God need permission from anyone, which is what "let" suggests to me.

John 1:4-5 replays the verse by saying of the *Logos*, "in him was life, and the life was the light of humanity. And the light shines in the darkness, and the darkness did not overtake it." John anticipates Jesus's self-identification in 8:12, "I am the light of the world." In John 9:5, Jesus repeats, "Whenever I am in the world, I am the light of the world." If John had access to Matthew, which I think is likely, then John 9:5 serves to underline the Sermon on the Mount, where Jesus tells his disciples, "You are the light of the world" (Matthew 5:14) and therefore they are to "let your light shine before other people, so that they may see your good works and glorify your Father in the heavens" (Matthew 5:16). The call is less that disciples "see light" than that they "be light": they are the light of the world. They are known by their good works.

The Bible is replete with images of light and dark—far too many to be contained in one chapter. Each image opens to multiple interpretations that prompt both reflection and action. The concern for light moves from the auditory to the visual, and it demonstrates both the complexity of creation as well as our own limited perceptions. Light refracts into multiple colors, with white light being polychromatic. Light is always more than what we can see: we cannot see ultraviolet or infrared, any more than we can hear sonic wavelengths. Thus, Jesus, the "light of the world" can only be understood, as Paul puts it in 1 Corinthians 13:12, through a "mirror dimly" or, in the King James Version, a "glass, darkly."

By speaking of Jesus as the "light of the world," John does more than evoke images of creation. Psalm 27:1 exults, "The Lord is my light and my salvation." The Hebrew translated "lord" is YHWH; in Greek, that name becomes *kyrios*, "lord," the title given to Jesus in the New Testament. When people in John's Gospel refer to Jesus as *kyrios*—the Samaritan woman in 4:11, 15, 19; the royal official in 4:49; the paralyzed man in 5:7; Simon Peter in 6:68; the woman convicted of adultery in 8:11; the man born blind in 9:36, 38; Mary and Martha in 11:3, and others—we readers need to determine what the force of the term is. Are the people addressing Jesus as "sir" and so being both polite and deferential, or are they acknowledging his cosmic sovereignty? The same question can be posed to any who address Jesus as "lord": are they saying what is expected of a Christian or are they recognizing divine rule and the light of the world? Taking "the name of the lord in vain" (Exodus 20:7; Deuteronomy 5:11) may be the most easily and frequently violated of the Decalogue, the Ten Words.

Jesus is for John the light of the world. According to Proverbs 6:23, "the commandment (Hebrew: *mitzvah*) is a lamp and the teaching (Hebrew: *torah*) a light." This intertextual connection suggests that for John, and so John's readers, Jesus and the Torah, including all the commandments, are inseparable. The earliest followers of Jesus were Jews (this should not be news), and so they both saw him in their Scriptures, from Genesis 1:1 on, and they interpreted him in light of those Scriptures. John's Prologue tells us, in multiple ways, that Jesus cannot be understood fully without knowledge of those earlier texts.

The light imagery continues to inform John's Gospel. In Isaiah 42:6, God states, "I, the Lord (YHWH), have called you in righteousness; I have taken you by your hand and I have kept you; I have given you as a covenant to the people, a light to the nations." The next verse, Isaiah 42:7, speaks of opening the eyes of the blind and so anticipates John 9, the healing of the man born blind.

Isaiah 42:1-6 is one of Isaiah's so-called "servant psalms" or "servant songs" (that term does not appear in the Scriptures; it was coined by the German Lutheran theologian Bernard Duhm in 1892), along with Isaiah 49:1-6; 50:4-11; and 52:13–53:12. In the Jewish tradition, this servant is the people Israel, the covenant community, as Isaiah 41:8 puts it, "And you, Israel, my servant, Jacob, whom I have chosen, the offspring (lit. 'seed') of Abraham, my friend" (see also Isaiah 44:1). The servant is the personification of Jewish community, taken into exile by the Babylonians in 587, harmed and humiliated, and then miraculously repatriated to the national homeland by Cyrus the Great in 538. The people who are redeemed are the Gentile nations, who witness the community's exile and then return, and so recognize the power of Israel's God.

The early followers of Jesus saw Jesus as this suffering servant, "pierced (or 'wounded') for our transgression (or 'rebellion'), crushed for our iniquities, upon him was the discipline that made us whole (or 'gave us peace'), and by his stripes (or 'blows') we are healed" (Isaiah 53:5). Perhaps Jesus himself identified with Isaiah's servant. John's Prologue connects Jesus to the servant not only by images of "light" but by the appeal in Isaiah to creation. Isaiah 42:5 reads, "Thus says God, the Lord (YHWH), who created the heavens and stretched them out, who spread out the earth and what comes from it, who gives breath (Hebrew: *neshama*; Greek: *pnoē*) to the people on it, and spirit (Hebrew: *ruach*, Greek: *pneuma*) to those who walk in it."

There are many other passages in the Old Testament that use light imagery. For example, Isaiah 60:19 anticipates the day when "the Lord will be an eternal light for you, and God will be your glory." In Micah 7:8 the prophet attests, "When I sit in darkness, the Lord is a light to me." Just as John's Gospel combines wind and breath and spirit so that when we feel a breeze, or a draft, we might sense the divine, so when we witness a sunrise, or turn on a lamp, the divine presence can be seen.

Christians here are in an excellent position to double dip. The Old Testament should not be seen as a checklist, so that each time a connection is made with Jesus, one can put a mark next to the verse and say, "Okay, done with this." A text can have, indeed should have, multiple meanings: what it meant to the people who first heard it; what it has meant over time since the Bible continues to speak to each generation anew; what it means to individual readers.

To bring light, to shine as light, whether the subject is Jesus or his followers, means more than just turning on a switch. It means being like God in the act of creation. It means changing what is to something that is better. It means bringing justice and teaching Torah. And that means attending to where justice is lacking: where poverty prevents people from living fully, where exploitation exists in place of equality, where corruption exists in place of community.

It means giving sight to the blind. Yes, we can take the point metaphorically and say that the light is what illumines our souls. But the point is also a practical one: it means health care for those who cannot see. Jesus literally gives sight to the blind. His comment in John 9, about how he is the light of the world as well as how "we" need to work in the light, comes immediately before he physically heals a beggar who had been born blind. Pedagogically, it means opening minds from the prisons of shortsightedness: it means seeing multiple perspectives, or understanding different wavelengths. We'll "see" more of the implications of these metaphors in chapters 3 and 4, where we meet the paralyzed man at the pool of Siloam and the man born blind.

After Jesus announces that he is the "light of the world" he immediately states in John 9:4, "It is necessary for us to work the works of the One who sent me while it is day; night is coming when no one is able to work." These works must be done while "it is day," while there is time to do it, for at some point it will be too late. John reminds me of a Jewish story, told by Rabbi Jacob Telushkin in his 2000 *Book of Jewish Values* (New York: Bell Tower, 2000).

The great rabbinic sage Rabbi Israel Salanter (1819–1883) was once spending the night at a shoemaker's home. Late at night, Salanter saw the man still working by the light of a flickering candle. Rabbi Salanter asked the man, "Look how late it is; your candle is about to go out. Why are you still working?" The shoemaker, undeterred by the rabbi's words, replied, "As long as the candle is burning, it is still possible to mend." For weeks afterward, Rabbi Salanter was heard repeating the shoemaker's words: "As long as the candle is burning, it is still possible to mend." The idea of mending, or repairing the world, is known in Judaism as *tikkun olam*; the expression can also mean "healing the world."

So how do we do this healing, this mending—how are we to "work the works" of God, especially in a world, a *kosmos*, where greed trumps generosity and selfishness trumps compassion? John's Gospel gives us several examples, of which two are most pertinent to images of light: Nicodemus, and the Samaritan woman at the well (whom we meet in chapter 2).

The Word Became Flesh

John 1:14 proclaims that the *Logos* became "flesh"—the Greek word for "flesh," *sarx*, conveys more than simply the idea of body, in Greek, *soma* (as in psychosomatic). *Sarx* also means human weakness, as in "the spirit is willing but the *sarx*, the flesh, is weak" (so Matthew 26:41 and Mark 14:38 in reference to the disciples who fail to keep watch with Jesus in Gethsemane). The Incarnation, the becoming flesh, means for John that the divine is embodied in Jesus of Nazareth. The following chapters give soundings (another aural term) on how to hear this Incarnation anew, through a few of the numerous stories John records.

In chapter 1, we stop at John 2:1-11 to attend a wedding at Cana and to witness the first of Jesus's signs, the turning of water into wine. The chapter not only introduces the mother of Jesus (never called "Mary" in the Fourth Gospel), it shows Jesus's enigmatic personality. Yes, he is rude to his mother, and yes, he listens to her.

Chapter 2 makes a brief stop at midnight for Jesus's conversation with Nicodemus (John 3) before turning to the story of the Samaritan at the well in John 4. Here our conversation includes the topics of sexuality and gender, law and judgment, and even implications for how we can be the light of the world when our vision is incomplete.

In chapter 3, we move to the healing of the (to me, annoying) paralyzed man at the pool in John 5 and in chapter 4 to the healing of the blind beggar in John 9. These accounts, unique to John's Gospel, not only open the conversation on the relationship between sin and disability, they also raise questions about personal, familial, and communal responsibility and the destructive power of rumors.

John 12 and 13, two stories of foot washing, are the subject of chapter 5. In the first, at a dinner, Mary the sister of Martha and Lazarus, anoints Jesus's feet; in the second, at a dinner, Jesus takes the role of an enslaved individual and washes the feet of his disciples. Together, the stories speak to matters of honor and shame, of friendship and family, even of the senses: sight and smell, touch and hearing.

As the two foot-washing stories interpret each other so that the whole is greater than the sum of the parts, the characters of Mary Magdalene and Doubting Thomas also interpret each other. In chapter 6, we find additional nuances to these two figures who interact with the resurrected Jesus. The stories return us to matters of hearing and sight as well as to questions of history and memory.

Our epilogue is breakfast with Jesus, John 21, an addition to the text that originally ended with John 20. Together with Peter, the Beloved Disciple, and a few others who shared this final meal with Jesus by the Sea of Galilee, we taste again the wine and the bread and see anew the incarnate word. We hear echoes of John the Baptizer and the Samaritan woman at the well, inhale the breath, the spirit, the stench of Lazarus's tomb and the perfume of Mary's ointment, and touch the memory of the man from Nazareth.

When John writes that the deeds of Jesus are too numerous to recount, he wasn't kidding. It would have been easy to fill an entire book just on the Prologue. For each chapter in this book, more can, and has, been written. There is so much more in John's Gospel—the other signs, the good shepherd, the Last Supper discourses—to savor. Let the Gospel open all your senses, feel it, touch it, taste it, see it, and above all listen to it. It has the potential to change the way we think, and when we change the way we think, we are better prepared to be a light to the world.

CHAPTER 1

The Wedding at Cana

(John 2)

John 1 sends us immediately back to "the beginning," to Genesis, and in returning to the beginning, the Gospel recreates the world. When John's readers encounter Genesis anew, they will see Jesus in the Word of God by which God creates the world and in the Light that God calls into being. As God in Genesis creates order out of chaos, so Jesus, by his various signs, does the same. The first sign, turning water into wine at a wedding in Cana, where the supply of wine had run out, is not the chaos of the primordial soup; it is not the destruction of war or the disorder of economic collapse. It is the personal chaos of social embarrassment, of a wedding that appears to be starting off on the wrong foot, and of a mother who nudges her reluctant son into action although it is not his time or, as Jesus puts it, his "hour has not yet come" (2:4).

The wedding scene also returns us to the beginning, this time to Genesis 2 and the creation of the figures we call Adam and Eve. These are not their names in Genesis 2, which only mentions, in Hebrew, *ha-adam*, "the earthling" and *ishah*, "woman." Nothing is said about marriage, and the couple, not yet knowing they are naked, would have no interest in wedding attire. There is no party, no gift table, no band or caterer. Nevertheless, later tradition understood this first couple as married, a point made clear in the Synoptic Gospels (Matthew, Mark, and Luke; called Synoptic because they "see together" in telling more-or-less the same story in the same order; John has a different chronology and different stories about Jesus, including the Cana wedding) where Jesus, in discussing divorce and remarriage, appeals to Genesis 2, "From the beginning (*archē*) of creation, [God] made them male and female. On account of this, a man shall leave his father and mother and cleave to his woman (the Greek *gynē* can also mean "wife"), and the two shall become one flesh (*sarx*).... Therefore, what God has joined together, let no one separate" (Mark 10:6-9).

John can even be understood as continuing to replay the plot of Genesis. In Genesis 3, the man and the woman eat the forbidden fruit (it only becomes an apple in the early Middle Ages) and seek to hide themselves from God. In John 3:20, Jesus tells Nicodemus, "All who do evil hate the light and do not come to the light, so that their works may not be exposed." John evokes Abraham ten times in chapter 8; Jacob in chapter 4; Moses in chapters 1, 3, 5, 6, 7, 8, and 9; the prophet Elijah in 1:21, 25; Isaiah in chapters 1 and 12; and so on.

The Scriptures of Israel are not John's only source; John also likely had access to the Synoptic Gospels. When I was in graduate school (when Noah was still on the ark), one of my professors insisted that John and the Synoptics were independent. Due in no small part to the work of my student James Barker, who is now a professor at Western Kentucky University, I've become increasingly convinced that John knows the Synoptic tradition and provides his own take on it. The idea of one evangelist (the technical term for a Gospel writer) retelling accounts from other evangelists is not new. Most biblical scholars, myself included, see Mark as a source for Matthew and Luke. In Luke 1:1-4, the evangelist notes that lots of people have attempted to write an orderly account of the story of Jesus based on information they received from eyewitnesses (thus Luke tells us that he was not on site), so he to seeks to present an orderly account. In other words, Luke had access to Mark and, probably, to Matthew, and Luke thought that he could do a better job.

My point is not that Mark was wrong. My point is that Matthew and Luke found Mark insufficient: no Nativity story, no Resurrection appearances, no Beatitudes or the "Our Father" prayer, and so on. Thus, Matthew and Luke supplemented Mark. John I think does the same to the Synoptic Gospels. Where there are potential problems, John sorts them. For example, in Luke 10:38-42, Mary and Martha never appear together, never speak to each other, and Martha remains upset with Mary's lack of support. In John 11–12, the two sisters work as a team. Family squabble in Luke becomes family solidarity in John.

The wedding at Cana seems to me to be another correction to a potential problem. In Matthew 19:12 Jesus praises individuals who "make themselves eunuchs for the sake of the kingdom of Heaven," an expression that commends those who do not procreate and, by extension, those who do not marry. In Mark 10:28 (followed by Matthew 19:27), Peter announces that he and the other members of Jesus's inner circle of twelve disciples have "left everything" to follow Jesus: that everything includes wives and children. Luke 18:29-30 depicts Jesus as teaching, "There is no one who has left house or wife or brothers [and sisters] or parents or children, for the sake of the kingdom of God, who will not get back very much more in this time (*kairos*), and in the eternity to come eternal life." Even Paul, in 1 Corinthians 7:9, expresses preference for the single rather than married life, "but if they [the Corinthians who follow Jesus] do not practice self-control (or cannot restrain themselves), they should marry, for it is better to marry than to burn [i.e., with passion]." John may well have felt the need to tell the followers that Jesus *did* approve of marriage, so much so that Jesus not only attended a wedding, he helped cater.

Alas, reception history (not "wedding reception" but how the tradition came to be understood) did not go in this pro-connubial direction. One early church legend casts the bride at the wedding as Mary Magdalene, stranded at the altar when Jesus calls the groom, the Beloved Disciple understood to be John, to be one of his followers. In John 2, we meet neither bride nor groom: we do not know how Jesus,

3

or his mother, knew them, if they were friends or relatives. For John 2, the bride and groom are not the most important people at the wedding. Nor are their parents. The focus is on Jesus, his mother, and the wine steward. I find this a helpful text when dealing with bridezillas, bachelor parties, controlling mothers and fathers, and everyone else who makes weddings annoying rather than enjoyable.

On the third day there was a wedding in Cana of Galilee, and the mother of Jesus was there. (John 2:1)

"On the third day" of what? John does not make this one easy for us. Back in 1:29, John mentions that "tomorrow" (most English translations read "the next day") John the Baptizer sees Jesus and announces, "Here is the lamb of God, the one who takes away (the Greek is literally "takes up") the sin of the world." The first day therefore must refer to the events earlier in the chapter, where the Baptizer testifies that he is not Elijah (in contradiction to the Synoptic tradition), not a prophet (again in contradiction) and finally not the Messiah. He is, quoting Isaiah 40, the forerunner who comes to announce the Messiah.

We can see a decrease in John's role as we move from the earliest Gospel, Mark, on to Matthew and Luke and finally John. According to Mark, John baptizes Jesus; Mark makes no comment about their relationship. In Matthew's version, John insists that because Jesus is his superior, it is Jesus who should be doing the baptism. Jesus insists that John perform the ritual, to "fulfill all righteousness" (Matthew 3:15; both "fulfill" and "righteousness" are signature Matthean terms). Matthew thus makes clear John's subordinate status. Luke increases the subordination by depicting John, while still a fetus, acknowledging, as his mother Elizabeth puts it, his "lord" (Luke 1:43). Finally, for John's Gospel, the Baptizer is no longer a prophet, or Elijah; he is merely a messenger. This subordination was necessary for the Gospel writers, since other people at the time saw John as a messianic figure. The Mandaeans still do.

John is doing more than counting off the days. When we return to the Scriptures of Israel, it turns out that the third day is the day when miracles occur. It would be great if John here alluded to Genesis 1, but this is not the case, at least directly. The "third day" (Genesis 1:13) is when God gathers the waters to create both seas and the dry land then creates vegetation.

The expression "the third day" occurs first in Genesis 22:4, when Abraham looked up and saw the "mountain of the Lord" (22:14) where he was to sacrifice his son Isaac. This connection, in retrospect, anticipates the sacrifice of Jesus, the beloved Son of God. In Jewish tradition, the location of the near sacrifice of Isaac is Mount Zion, the future location of the Temple (see 2 Chronicles 3:1 which mentions Mount Moriah). Other momentous events on the third day include the manifestation of God on Mount Sinai and the giving of the Torah (Exodus 19:11), and Hosea 6:2 where the prophet exhorts the people Israel to return to the Lord (Hebrew: YHWH; Greek: *kyrios*), for "after two days he will revive us (i.e., bring us to life), and on the third day he will raise us up, that we may live before him." For Jesus's followers, he is a new Isaac, he is a new Moses, and he is the one who is raised, so that those who follow him will be raised as well.

More, it will be on the third day that Jesus, according to the Gospels, will be raised from the tomb (Matthew 16:21; 17:23; 20:19; Luke 9:22; 18:33; 24:7, 46; Acts 10:40; 1 Corinthians 15:4). Notably, his Passion prediction does not occur in John's Gospel. John, with knowledge of the Synoptics, and we readers today with that same knowledge, did not need to have Jesus make a Passion prediction. Here the evangelist again clues the readers: the more you know of your Scripture, both the Scriptures of Israel and the other Gospels, the deeper your appreciation of John's narrative becomes.

In John 2, this third day is not the day of Jesus's resurrection; it is a wedding. To this point in the Gospel, we have met John the Baptizer and, in John 1, Jesus encounters the first of his disciples. There is no baptism of Jesus in the Fourth Gospel, which is another part of its subordination of the baptizer to Jesus. Why foreground a wedding?

There are multiple answers, aside from the obvious one that we biblical scholars, so intrigued by intertextual allusions, often fail to notice. First, it is possible that Jesus went to a wedding in Cana. He could have easily traveled there from Nazareth, which is about nine miles to the south. Nevertheless, Jesus did lots of things that are not recorded in any Gospel, so again, why a wedding? Here are six more of many possible answers.

Second, as already suggested, John may be controlling the Synoptic narratives that appear to downplay marriage and family in favor of fictive kinships. People in the Synoptic traditions leave their families to follow Jesus, and Jesus in these texts, as well as Paul in 1 Corinthians, promotes celibacy over marriage. By depicting Jesus at a wedding, John affirms marriage.

Third, while the wedding is not that of Jesus himself, the wedding imagery should remind us of the tradition of Jesus as a bridegroom and his followers as "sons of the wedding hall" or, more mundanely, "wedding guests" (see Matthew 9:15; Mark 2:19-20; Luke 5:34-35). The parable of the wise and foolish virgins in Matthew 25:1-13 draws on the same images. That Jesus is a "bridegroom" indicates that to be in his presence is like being at a wedding, with celebration, with food, with the promise of a new family. In John's Gospel, Jesus does not refer to himself as a bridegroom, but John the Baptizer accords him this role: in John 3:29, the Baptizer explains, "The one who has the bride is the bridegroom, and the friend (Greek: *philos*, as in "Philadelphia") of the bridegroom, the one who stands and hears him, rejoices greatly at the bridegroom's voice. For this reason my joy has been fulfilled." For John's Gospel, the followers of Jesus are not just disciples, they are "friends" (*philoi*, John 15:14) when they do what Jesus commands them and because he has informed them about everything he has heard from his Father (15:15). He proves his friendship in his crucifixion, since as he states in 15:13 (KJV), "Greater love hath no man than this, that a man lay down his life for his friends" (*philoi*).

The fourth explanation is related to the third: the image of Jesus as bridegroom draws upon the motif in Israel's Scriptures of God as the bridegroom and then husband of Israel. The metaphor thus casts Jesus's followers in the role of the bride. Similar images appear in Paul's letters, such as 2 Corinthians 11:2, where the apostle, speaking to his Gentile *ekklēsia* (the term, meaning "assembly" and usually translated "church," is in Greek a feminine noun), states, "I am zealous for you with a zeal of God, for I promised you in marriage to one husband, to present you as a pure virgin to the Christ." Similarly, in Revelation 21:2, the seer proclaims, "And the holy city, the new Jerusalem, I saw, coming down out of heaven from God, prepared as a bride adorned for her husband," who is the Christ.

Fifth, the wedding imagery, with its abundance of wine, is a foretaste of the messianic banquet, when "The Lord of hosts will make for all the peoples on this mountain a feast of rich food, a feast of well-aged wines, of rich food filled with marrow, of well-aged wines strained clear" (Isaiah 25:6). The Dead Sea Scrolls, several passages in the New Testament, and Rabbinic literature all display a literary technique in which a cited verse signals that the reader should look at that verse's immediate context. Isaiah 25:6 is connected to John 2 given the touchstones of wine and of Jesus's messianic role. The connection is enhanced when we realize that Isaiah 25:8 proclaims that God "will swallow up death forever"; the next chapter proclaims, "Your dead will live, my corpse will rise" (Isaiah 26:19). When we know the context of the allusion to Isaiah, John's text becomes all the more profound.

Sixth, wedding imagery anticipates other scenes in the Gospel, from the discussion of marriage between Jesus and the Samaritan woman in John 4 in which Jesus acts the part of the bridegroom, to the depiction of Mary Magdalene as a lost lover at the tomb in John 20.

And seventh, weddings are the start of new families. According to Genesis 2, as we have seen, a man leaves his father and mother and cleaves to his wife, and thus a new family begins. John's Gospel creates new families as well, based on leaving father and mother and becoming a new creation. In the Gospel's next chapter, Jesus explains to Nicodemus that one must be "born anew" or "born from above" (John 3:7).

The last phrase of John 2:1 introduces "the mother of Jesus." We know from the Synoptic Gospels and Acts that her name is Mary. For John, the focus is not on her name—which given both Mary the sister of Martha and Mary from Magdala (or perhaps Mary the Tower), can make for a confusing narrative—but on her role as mother. She is the mother of Jesus, but she will also become, in John 20, the new mother of the similarly unnamed Beloved Disciple. That she has other children, whom we meet at the wedding, shows the importance of this new family: Jesus entrusts his mother not to her other biological children, but to the Beloved Disciple.

John's Gospel gives us no nativity account, nothing about a virginal conception, magi, or shepherds, not even a birth in Bethlehem. In fact, the Prologue seems to erase the need for a mother. Jesus is, according to the Prologue, both God and with God; he is the perfect image of God the Father. Thus, for John's Gospel, when people see Jesus, it is as if they are seeing God. This perfect likeness between a son and a father can indicate that the mother has made no contribution to the appearance or nature of the child. For John, Jesus is this perfect likeness. From such a view easily follows the claim, from the second-century group known as Valentinians, that Jesus passed through Mary like water through a tube. John insists both on the Incarnation, the taking on of flesh, so that Jesus is not a type of friendly spirit (I am reminded of the old cartoon character Casper the Friendly Ghost, who I for a while confused with one of the magi). Thus, Mary is needed to ground Jesus in his humanity. However, because there is no description of the conception and birth, the mother of Jesus is

8

important in John's Gospel because of what she does, not because of the particulars of her biology.

Jesus and his disciples were also called to the wedding. (John 2:2)

There are verses that demand attention and that remain in memory. Then there's John 2:2. Compared to the wealth of commentary on other passages in the Gospel, John 2:2 gets short shrift. Personally, I like this verse a lot, since it opens space for both imagination and action.

The first verse of the chapter focuses on Jesus's mother, so that the reference to Jesus and the disciples comes as an afterthought: yes, he and his friends were there too. While the disciples get a shout-out, John makes no mention here of Jesus's "brothers and sisters." No reference to Joseph here or anywhere else in John, for whom the only father to Jesus is God.

Nor are we told who called, or invited them: the bride or her family, the groom or his family? Did the mother of Jesus ask for them to be invited, and did she ask that the disciples be included? Such inclusion may sound odd to twenty-first-century ears: If I am invited to a wedding, I would not expect my children to be invited if they did not know the couple, let alone for my graduate students to come along. We do know from later rabbinic sources that a man's (yes, this is a patriarchal culture) disciples were like his sons, so it is possible that the disciples would be seen as part of the family and so included in an invitation. To this point, Jesus only has a few disciples, and only in chapter 6 (vv. 67, 70, 71), at the feeding of the five thousand, does John mention, in an offhand way that suggests readers knew the tradition of the "twelve" from the Synoptics, that Jesus had twelve disciples. John 20:24, the only other reference to the number, mentions that "Thomas, one of the Twelve, who was called 'the twin,'" was not present when Jesus first appeared, after his resurrection, to his followers. A few disciples will not overburden the people paying for the wedding. Moreover, as far as we can determine from both written and archaeological remains, lower Galilee at the time of Jesus was relatively prosperous. There should have been enough food for the village, and a few more guests.

We have very little information about weddings in Galilee in the early first century CE, so the best we can do is extrapolate from general village customs. Weddings in villages, and Cana is a relatively small village, were often communal affairs where everyone joined in the celebration. Instead of the regular diet of fish from the Sea of Galilee, vegetables, olives, cheese, and wine, it is likely that meat— likely from a sheep or, if the family is very upscale, a "well-fed calf" (see Luke 15:23)—would be part of the menu.

Pastorally, the verse strikes me as helpful for any church wedding. After the "important" parts of the wedding are sorted—the outfits for the wedding party, rings, flowers, caterer, band, and so on—do the people who insist on a church wedding think about inviting Jesus and his disciples? Is the ceremony only for friends, or are all members of the congregation invited? If the church is not part of the lives of the wedding couple or their parents, what is the point of getting married in a church at all? What would it mean for Christians to think about inviting Jesus to the wedding? A house of worship, be it a church, a synagogue, a mosque, and so on, should be more than a destination venue.

All members of a congregation can and do attend baptisms and bar and bat mitzvahs, which are part of the worship services, respectively, in churches and synagogues. All members of a congregation can attend funerals. If a wedding is to be held in a church, why not invite the congregation to the ceremony?

And when the wine was lacking, the mother of Jesus says to him, "They have no wine." (John 2:3)

The mother does not ask a question or make a demand; she uses a form of speech known as an "indirect request." We see the same rhetorical move in John 11:3, when Mary and Martha send word to Jesus about Lazarus, "Lord, look! The one whom you love is ill." The mother expects Jesus to do something about the wine, just as the sisters expect Jesus to do something about their ailing brother. When I mention to my son, "Your sister's birthday is in two weeks," I am not simply conveying information; I expect him to send a card. Statements can easily be requests; our task is to determine how the statements function.

Since this rhetorical form is so popular, it is even more striking in John's Gospel when someone makes a direct request. For example, when Jesus meets the woman at the well, he could have said, "I am thirsty," which would have conveyed to her that she should do something about it, such as using her bucket to draw him some water. Instead, he demands, "Give me to drink" (John 4:7). When do we make a statement, and when do we demand? The statement form allows us to respond variously, from "yes, I should do something about it" to "so what?" or "why are you telling me this?" The demand forecloses the options.

For one more iteration of this form, in John 19:28, as Jesus hangs on the cross, he says, "I thirst." This is not just a statement of fact; it is an indirect request. Jesus thirsts, not simply for something to drink, but to be in communion with his followers. And in this last request, we return from the cross to Cana, where the mother of Jesus has informed him that people do not have wine to drink; we return from the cross to the town of Sychar in Samaria, where Jesus demanded something to drink and then told the woman that "whoever would drink of the water that I will give them will never thirst" (John 4:14). In between these earlier stories and the cross, John emphasizes drinking in chapter 6, and again in the feeding of the five thousand, which for John's Gospel is also the bread of life discourse. There Jesus instructs his followers, "Unless you eat the flesh (*sarx*) of the Son of Humanity and drink his blood, you have no life in you" (John 6:53; see also 6:54-56). Finally, in 18:11, Jesus speaks about drinking metaphorically, when he asks Peter, "The cup that the Father gave me, shall I not drink it?"

Reading through John, we should become thirsty, and we should experience multiple tastes, fine wine, the bitter cup, living water.

And Jesus said to her, "What to me and to you, woman? My hour has not yet come." (John 2:4)

There is no way to make this verse sound anything but rude. Claims that "men usually called their mothers 'woman'" have no support. The insistence that Jesus spoke to his mother with a smile on his lips and a twinkle in his eye, an insistence that is also evoked to explain his comment to the Canaanite woman in Matthew 15:26, "It is not good to take the children's bread and throw it to the puppies," makes little sense of either comment. Jesus is many things, but in these two episodes, he is not a twinkly sort of person.

"What to me and to you?" is an idiom that means "what business is that of either yours or mine?" or, more crassly, the expression ranges from "not my problem" to "butt out." The same expression appears in Mark 5:7 (see also Luke 8:28), when the demons named "legion" cry out, "What to me and to you, Jesus, Son of the Most High God? I implore you by God, do not torture me." A version of it, "what to us and to you?" appears in Mark 1:24, where again a demon cries out, "What to us and to you, Jesus of Nazareth? Have you come to destroy us? I know who you are, the Holy One of God." In John, it is Jesus, not the demons, who uses the expression.

The Septuagint, the Greek translation of the Scriptures of Israel, uses the expression in cases of serious disagreement. For example, in Judges 11:12, the hero, Jephthah, sends messengers to the king of the Ammonites to ask, "what between you and me, that you have come to me to fight against my land?" (2 Chronicles 35:21 gives another example of the expression in relation to war). In 1 Kings 17:18, the widow of Zarephath asks the prophet Elijah, "What between me and you, man of God? You have come to me to cause my sin to be remembered and to cause the death of my son." For one more example, in 2 Kings 3:13, the king of Judah, Jehoshaphat (yes, as in "jumping"), together with the kings of Israel and Edom, seeks out the prophet Elisha. The prophet, not interested in their alliances, responds to the king of Israel, "What to me and to you? Go to your father's prophets or to your mothers." In other words, "whatever you want is not my job" or, in restaurant-speak, "you're not at my table."

John replays here Mark 3:31-33, where Jesus's "mother and his brothers" seek him, and Jesus responds to the messengers that "whoever does the will of God, this one is my brother and sister and mother" (Mark 3:35). Lest readers familiar with the Synoptic tradition get the impression that Jesus has dismissed his family of origin, John shows in 2:4 the distance from the mother, but then in the rest of chapter 2 and again in chapter 19, at the cross, shows that the distance is fully transcended.

The address "woman" rather than "mother" distances Jesus from his mother. In terms of parental language, he will only acknowledge his "Father." Yet Jesus uses the same address in speaking to the Samaritan woman at the well (John 4:21), to his mother again at the cross (19:26), and to Mary Magdalene at the tomb (20:15). While we could conclude that all women look alike to Jesus, I find it more helpful to see the title as emphasizing the role that women play in the Gospel. The story cannot be told without them. More, although the address is the same, the characters of the mother of Jesus, the Samaritan woman, and Mary Magdalene show different personalities and different ways of relating to Jesus: as mother, as friend and collaborator, and as (chaste) lover.

Jesus's comment, "my hour has not yet come," drives toward the cross. From the chapter's opening comment "the third day" to the reference to the hour in verse 4, and throughout the Gospel, time takes on additional meaning. In 4:23, Jesus tells the Samaritan woman, "But the hour is coming, and is now, when the true worshipers will worship the Father in spirit and truth, for the Father seeks such as these worshiping him." For the followers of Jesus to whom John writes, any time they worship is that hour, that momentous time.

13

In John 5:25, Jesus announces, "the hour is coming, and is now, when the dead will hear the voice of the Son of God, and those who hear will live." The raising of Lazarus in John 11 becomes the fulfillment, in part, of this notice. Biblical scholars will sometimes use the expression, the "already/not yet," to refer to time in the Gospels. The time of Jesus, which is for the Gospels the time of the messianic age, is already here.

However, the time of a general resurrection of the dead, a final judgment, of peace on earth, or what the followers of Jesus came to call the *Parousia* (Greek: "appearance") or "second coming," has not yet occurred. John keeps readers in this state of already-not-yet-ness. Eternal life, or life abundant, or salvation can be experienced in the encounter with Jesus, and yet there is still disease, still death, and still more to come. The technical term for this both/and situation is "realized eschatology," in which the benefits of the end time, the eschaton, are realized in the present. And that's enough technical terminology for one chapter.

In John 7:30, Jesus is about to be arrested, but he escapes because, the narrator observes, "his hour had not yet come." In the so-called Last Supper discourses, where Jesus talks, a lot, to his disciples, he tells them that previously he had been using figures of speech (such as using different meanings for "spirit/wind," "running water/living water," being born anew versus being born again). Then he makes clear, "The hour is coming what I will no longer speak to you in figures, but I will report to you with freedom of speech (Greek: *parrēsia*, which also has the connotation of "boldly") about the Father" (John 16:25). This verse is John's version of Mark 8:31-32a, the "confession at Caesarea Philippi," where Peter proclaims Jesus to be the Christ, and Jesus, instead of speaking in parables, "began to teach them that it is necessary for the Son of Humanity to undergo much suffering, and be rejected by the elders and the chief priests and the scribes, and be killed, and after three days to rise. And he spoke the word (*logos*) with freedom of speech (Greek: *parrēsia*). For Mark, the christological focus is on Jesus's suffering and death; for John, it is on Jesus's and the Father's mutual glorification. Thus, in John 17:1 Jesus raises his eyes to heaven and says, "Father, the hour has come." The hour, which he knows and controls, is the time for mutual glorification: "Glorify your Son," says Jesus, "so that the Son may glorify you."

John 16 does speak about suffering, but here the suffering is less what Jesus will face than what John predicts his followers will face: "An hour is coming when all who kill you will suppose that they are offering worship to God" (John 16:2b).

In John's Gospel, time is ordered not chaotic, from the big bang of John 1:1 to the end of history. Jesus will be arrested on his own time, at his own hour. At his own hour, and not by the plans of anyone else, will he die and will he be raised. Because the countdown in John, which began in 1:1 with the big bang, is assured, day to day, then hour to hour, readers can also be assured that predictions yet to be fulfilled will also have their appropriate day and hour.

Greek has two words for time: *chronos* (as in chronology) is clock time, or lunchtime, or cocktail hour. *Kairos* is opportune time, not just moment, but momentous. In John's Gospel, the two types of time intertwine. When we look at a watch, or a clock, or when someone asks, "What time is it?" the Gospel suggests that each minute could be not just *chronos* but *kairos*. Just as reading John's Gospel brings new sensations to taste and touch, so it brings new meaning to time. It gives every day, every hour, new meaning; it makes time count.

His mother said to the servants, "What he tells you, do." (John 2:5)

I like Jesus's mother (one Jewish mother to another): she knows her son. Despite his rudeness, his dismissal of her concern, she knows that he will do what she indirectly requests he do. Instead of fussing at him ("Young man, that is no way to talk to your mother!") she simply turns to the "servants" (Greek: *diakonoi*, whence "deacons") and tells them to listen to him.

John, writing toward the end of the first century, would have known of the church office of deacons. In Romans 16:1, Paul mentions a woman named Phoebe, who is a "deacon of the assembly (*ekklēsia*) at Cenchreae, which is the port of Corinth. She is likely the person who brought his letter to Rome. Philippians 1:1 presumes that both bishops and deacons are in place to guide the congregations; 1 Timothy 3:8-13 provides a list of qualifications for the office of deacons. For John 2, deacons are people who (a) serve others, (b) listen to Jesus, and (c) listen to *women*. These deacons, servants in John 2, likely included both men and women, since the Greek masculine plural can include women.

The only other time John mentions the verb *diakoneō* is at 12:26, where Jesus states, "Whoever serves me must follow me, and where I am, there will my servant be also. Whoever serves me, the Father will honor." The Synoptic Gospels do not call the disciples *diakonoi*, servants or even deacons in the sense of an ecclesial office. Perhaps John, working on a more egalitarian model than the Epistles, sees all people who "serve Jesus" to be not just servants, but deacons.

John could have described these attendants as "enslaved," and enslaved people appear elsewhere in the Gospel (see, e.g., 4:51, the enslaved individuals who report a healing to the royal official; 18:10 on Malchus, enslaved to the High Priest). Perhaps at this wedding, this time of celebration, this foretaste of the messianic banquet, everyone is free, and safe, and happy. The picture is a contrast to the various "wedding parables" in the Synoptic Gospels, which usually include enslaved characters, and which always end badly (for example, the parable of the wedding banquet in Matthew 22:1-14). There are no parables in John's Gospel, but there are stories that evoke images of the parables recorded elsewhere. Thank you, John, for telling a story of a wedding with a very happy ending.

There were standing there six stone water jars for purification [washings] of the Jews, each holding twenty or thirty gallons [lit: measures]. (John 2:6)

Here's where much Christian interpretation goes wonky. I find, frequently, in commentaries and especially in sermons, the claim that by turning water into wine, Jesus "replaces" or "eliminates" Jewish practices concerning purification, which the commentator or homilist then concludes represent law rather than grace, or external legalism versus internal and sincere purification. Nonsense. The six stone jars tell us many things, but the elimination or, worse, degrading of Jewish practice is not one of them.

The stone in question is chalkstone or limestone, and chalkstone vessels have been and continue to be found in archaeological digs throughout lower Galilee. Unlike ceramic jars, stone vessels are impervious to impurity, since the liquid, if it becomes impure (for example, a dead rat falls into it—with apologies for this image), does not permeate the stone as it would pottery. The vessels are also less likely to break. The use of chalkstone vessels, along with aniconic coins, Sabbath lamps (which did not require additional lighting on Friday night, the start of the Sabbath), ritual bathing pools, and so on, were all means by which Jews celebrated their distinctive way of life, despite the incursion of Roman culture under Herod the Great and his son, the tetrarch of Galilee Herod Antipas. The tradition of washing before eating, which is still practiced by Orthodox Jews, is related to the Pharisees' extension of priestly privileges beyond the priesthood and outside of the Temple, to all Jews, since Israel is to be a "kingdom of priests and a holy nation" (Exodus 19:6).

Jesus is not doing away with this tradition, since he, and his disciples, and his mother, and everyone else would have already washed. The meal is in full swing, so much so that all the wine has been consumed. This is why Jesus instructs the servants to "fill" the vessels.

The vessels not only tell us that the setting is a Jewish wedding, they also give a sense of the size. Thirty gallons sounds like a lot, at least to me, but I admit to looking up what this would be in equivalent measures. A keg of beer is a little over fifteen gallons. Therefore, if my math is correct, each vessel is the equivalent of two kegs of beer. Therefore, the wine Jesus provides is about 12 kegs or, for those who do not drink alcohol, about 216,000 venti-size coffees. This is a big party.

That John must explain what these vessels are suggests that his intended audience, or at least a part of it, are not Jews. John has to explain Jewish customs. John writes for the readers of Matthew, Mark, and Luke, and for any other follower of Jesus, Jewish, Gentile, or Samaritan.

Jesus says to them, "Fill the jars with water." And they filled them up to the brim. And he says to them, "Now draw [some] out, and bring [it] to the catering manager." So they brought it. (John 2:7-8)

As his mother advised, so the servants do: they follow Jesus's instructions to "Fill the jars with water" (thus indicating that there was no water left, for everyone had already washed prior to the meal), and they do so "to the brim." They "fulfill" his instructions. We can think of this as topping off.

My translation of the Greek *architriklinos* as "catering manager" updates the usual "head steward" or "chief steward." *Archi* means "chief" or "prime" and a triclinium is a Roman-style formal dining room; it takes its name from the low dining table shaped like three ("tri") sides of a square or rectangle, with couches along each side.

Weirdly, or at least weird to me, the servants do not ask why Jesus asks them to fill the jars (which would have taken some time) or to bring the contents to the manager. Given that the problem is lack of wine, not lack of water, they might have expected (okay, I would have expected) him to have them fill up the wineskins or, given the size of the party, the jars in which the wine was kept.

Nor does John tell us what the servants saw when they brought out "some" and took it to the manager. Was it already wine? Did it change on the way?

The attendants have a story that we must fill in for ourselves. The mother of Jesus told them, "Do whatever he tells you," and they do. Are they merely following orders, or do they have "faith"? Do they realize the import of what is about to happen, and of their role in it? Did they taste the wine themselves? Were they offered a place at the table? At the least, they do remind me of the people who provide support in restaurants and banquets. With all the excitement over the really good wine, did anyone say "Thank you"?

And when the catering manager tasted the water that had become wine, and did not know where it came from (but the servants (diakonoi) who had drawn the water knew), the catering manager calls the bridegroom and says to him, "All people first put out the good wine, and when the guests have become drunk then [they put out] the inferior wine. You have kept the good wine until now." (John 2:9-10)

The story has the sense of a magic trick, performed then and now, when one liquid is exchanged for another. Videos explain how to do "magic merlot" or to turn water into wine: gradually allow water to drip into a glass of wine: the water, which has a higher density, sinks to the bottom of the glass, while the wine, which is lighter, rises to the top. Skeptics can thus explain away the miracle. I can imagine ancient storytellers doing this trick while recounting John 2: the wonder will remain, just as professional magicians amaze today, even when we know how they performed the trick.

People in antiquity might have done the same. Miracles look very much like magic, with the distinction often being in the eye of the beholder. What is a miracle to one person is magic to another. But this type of scientific explanation, where Jesus changes the atomic composition of liquid, is not John's point. Doubters will doubt, regardless of who tells the story, or who performs the miracle. John's Gospel depicts Jesus as performing seven signs, and each one is more magnificent: (1) turning water into wine (2:1-12); (2) the healing from a distance of the royal official's son, John's replay in 4:46-54 of the healing of the centurion's enslaved boy in Matthew 8:5-13 and Luke 7:1-10; (3) the healing of the paralyzed man (5:1-11), a replay of the Synoptic story of the healing of the paralyzed man let down through the roof; (4) the feeding of the five thousand, which John combines with the bread of life discourse (6:1-15); (5) walking on water (6:16-21); (6) healing the man born blind (9:1-12); and (7) raising Lazarus from the dead (chap. 11). Each sign for John has its own symbolic meaning.

Turning water into wine anticipates the messianic banquet, as we have seen. More, just as John 1 shows that Jesus outranks John the Baptizer, who insists in John 1:30 and 3:30, that Jesus is more important than he is, so John 2 depicts Jesus as greater than another rival. This time the evangelist makes the comparison not by the pronouncement of a character in the Gospel, but by symbolism John's initial audience would understand. By turning water into wine, Jesus outranks another god, also known as a "son of a god," who dies and rises again; this other god, also known for having women followers, was particularly associated with wine. This god, whom Jesus outranks, is known as Dionysus in the Greek-speaking world, and in Rome as Bacchus.

When John tells us that the manager "called the bridegroom," we should pause, since the reference could be to the actual man who got married at Cana, the one responsible for the wine, or it could be to Jesus, identified throughout the tradition as the bridegroom. Which bridegroom do we choose to see, and which bridegroom should get the credit for the good wine?

Finally, we might query the catering manager's view regarding what gets served when. For the manager, the host would serve the best first, and when taste buds are dulled along with other senses from alcohol intake, then comes the plonk. Thus, the manager is surprised that the best was left for last. The point strikes me as economical, but also tacky. Nor do we have any evidence from antiquity of people actually engaging in this practice. In fact, wine tasting programs typically start with the lighter wines first, and move to the more complex, with the lighter wines being the less expensive and the more complex the pricier. Then again, John is writing a Gospel, not copy for the Napa Valley.

Jesus did this, the first of his signs (Greek: sēmeia, as in semiotics), in Cana of Galilee, and revealed his glory; and his disciples believed in him. (John 2:11)

The gaps in this story, one on top of the next, leave me disoriented, as if I've consumed a lot of that rich wine at Cana. I thought I knew what was going on: the wedding ran out of wine, Jesus's mother indirectly requested that Jesus do something, then she tells the servants to follow his instructions. They fill six stone jars to the brim with water, and take some.... And here I'm lost. Some what? Water? Wine? A liquid that shifts from water to wine as they are transporting it? The servants bring the—what? water? wine?—to the catering manager, but now he's confused, since the servants knew where the—what? water? wine?—came from but he did not. He calls the bridegroom: Who? Jesus? The fellow getting married? He speaks of saving the best for last, which suggests at the least that the custom normally followed was tacky. And now, a reference to a "sign"—meaning what? Sign of what? Why not just use the Greek term *dynamis*, "mighty work" or "miracle"?

I'm still confused, or tipsy. Jesus "revealed his glory": How? To whom? Did the servants know that he changed water into wine? If so, why did they not believe? Or are these servants, these *diakonoi*, these "deacons" also disciples? They do what Jesus tells them to do, and that is what disciples are supposed to do. Unlike the Synoptics, John rarely

21

talks about the Twelve, as we have seen, and never provides a list of names. Who is, in John's view, among the disciples?

More, what exactly do these disciples "believe"? That Jesus can turn water into wine (so can Penn and Teller)? That he is another Dionysus? That he is more than Dionysus? Or, since the Greek verb translated "believed," *pisteō*, can also mean "had faith in" or "trusted," perhaps John is emphasizing the trustworthiness of what Jesus does, from listening to his mother even though it was not his time to manifest this glory, to helping the wedding planners avoid social embarrassment, to increasing the joy of everyone who attended the wedding. On the matter of signs, as the introduction notes, John finds even "more blessed" those who do not see and yet believe, so are the signs needed?

John will help us regain our balance, although there's something about the Gospel that remains, well, heady. When Jesus announces in John 15:1, "I am the true vine, and my Father is the vine grower [lit: farmer]," we will remember the wedding at Cana. As Jesus is dying, some people by the cross put a sponge full of sour wine on a branch of hyssop and hold it to his lips. Jesus receives the wine and then, fully aware and in control, announces, "It is finished" (John 19:29-30). Again, we remember the taste of the rich wine at the wedding, and we know that the rich wine will replace the sour wine, just as the living body of Jesus will replace the corpse.

CHAPTER 2

Nicodemus and the Samaritan Woman at the Well

(John 3 & 4)

Entire books have been written on Nicodemus and the Samaritan woman. To make this chapter manageable, we focus on two of the many subjects that unite the accounts. First is the use of language, for example, how do we distinguish being born again, which means crawling back into the mother's womb, from being born anew, or born from above? Or how do we tell the difference between running water and living water, since again, the terms are the same? Or again, what do we do when ordinary words, such as wells and buckets, springs and fountains, can also be the language of both fertility and flirtation? Second is the question of judging not only when we do not have all the facts but also when understanding requires not just rational thought but also divine revelation: why is Nicodemus in the dark while the Samaritan woman is in the light?

The two chapters, John 3 and 4, can stand on their own, but the comparison of the stories of these very different people who encounter Jesus provides insight into questions of gender and sexuality, reason and revelation, humanity and Christology.

Being Reborn and Receiving the Spirit

According to John 3, Nicodemus, a "leader of the Jews" (3:1), comes to Jesus at midnight. He's in the dark, clueless, struggling to gain understanding and probably afraid of what his association with Jesus might convey to his fellow Pharisees who resist Jesus's teaching. I appreciate his willingness to pursue what he finds interesting and important; however, his stealthy approach remains for me a problem. It takes courage to admit what we do not know and to seek answers; it may take even more courage to let others know that we are seeking, that we do not know everything, that we may need help.

Jesus does not make matters easy for Nicodemus. As elsewhere in the Gospel, this Word-made-flesh takes vocabulary, words, out of their mundane, fleshy, meaning and moves them toward the transcendent.

At the beginning of their conversation, Jesus says to Nicodemus, "Amen, Amen, I say to you..." (John 3:3a), which most English translations render as "very truly." Sigh.... The translation misses the impact of the words. Most people end sentences and especially prayers, with "amen," which comes from the Hebrew word meaning "so be it." Jesus not only starts with "amen," he repeats the term (as at the end of prayers in Nehemiah 8:6; Tobit 8:8; and Judith 13:20). To begin with "amen" is topsy-turvy; "so be it," a wish and a hope, becomes "it is thus," a statement of fact.

While Nicodemus is working his way through the amens, Jesus continues, "No one is able to see the kingdom of God..." (3:3b)— and we stop here again. While the Synoptic Gospels spend a lot of time talking about the "kingdom of God," especially in relation to the parables, John does not. In fact, John has no formal "parables" and does not even use the term. John only speaks about this kingdom here in 3:3 and again in 3:5, and that's it. What is this kingdom? It is possible, and I think likely, that John had access to the Synoptic Gospels and so did John's readers. Therefore, John adverts to these earlier texts: you thought parables were hard to understand? Nicodemus is experiencing the same disorientation that the parables create.

The kingdom is not something that can be "seen" or even "heard" but it can be sensed; it can be experienced. It is that moment when what is important is understood with clarity; when feelings of calm, of peace, of comprehension wash over us, when we recognize our vocation, what we are supposed to do.

As if the "amen, amen" and "the kingdom of God" were not difficult enough, Jesus sandwiches between the two expressions the qualification, "without being born *anōthen*." I left the final word in Greek because the Greek term has multiple connotations: from above, anew, and again. There is a pun here, which works only in Greek and not in Hebrew. My conservative Christian friends see Jesus as capable of speaking in all languages; my liberal Christian friends suggest that John invented this pun to help explain how joining the community gathered in Jesus's name replaces the natal family. Thus, they see it as consistent with Jesus's mission while not being his actual words.

Here's how the pun functions. *Anōthen* can mean "again," as we see in Galatians 4:9, where Paul asks his audience: "Now that you know God, or rather have come to be known by God, why would you turn back again to the weak and poor elements?" Paul is talking about the supernatural forces that all people—Jews, Samaritans, and Gentiles—understood to be impacting behavior. He puts the issue bluntly, "How can you want to be enslaved to them again (*anōthen*)?" That "again" is how Nicodemus takes the term *anōthen*, and therefore he asks Jesus, "How is a person able be born after having grown old? A person is not able to enter her mother's womb a second time and be born."

"Born again" is thus not a good translation of John's language, despite the popularity of the term today. Jesus is speaking of another meaning, "from above." Again, he is playing with language and so helping both Nicodemus, and the reader, to see and think in other terms. "From above" can simply mean "from the top." For example, Matthew 27:51 and Mark 15:38 both describe the Temple curtain as being torn "from top [*anōthen*] to bottom." The term can also mean "from the first," as in Luke 1:3, where the evangelist states that he had investigated everything carefully "from the first" or "from the beginning" (*anōthen*).

We are getting to the meaning of Jesus's comment, but we need one more step. "The top" or "the first" can also refer to "up there," that is, heaven. Aha! Jesus is not talking about being born again, but being born "from above," by being called by God and responding. In 3:31, he tells Nicodemus, "The one who comes from above (*anōthen*) is above all." Here he is talking about himself. And in John 19:11a, Jesus tells Pontius Pilate, the Roman governor, "you would have no power over me unless it had been given to you *anōthen*, from above."

Nicodemus is thinking literally, and the Johannine Jesus wants him to think metaphorically. Nicodemus thinks one-dimensionally, and the Johannine Jesus wants him to think in multiple dimensions.

I'm finding myself increasingly sympathizing with Nicodemus. At the same time, and to me disturbing, I'm finding myself thinking that I know more than he does. I understand the puns that so confuse poor Nicodemus. Such a feeling can be one of superiority, or chosenness, or being special, in that we know the secret codes that others cannot fathom. At the same time, this sense of being in on the secret is elitist. Thanks John: it's hard to be humble when one knows the secret.

Jesus elaborates with another "Amen amen" statement in 3:5, "Amen amen I say to you, no one is able to enter the Kingdom of God without being born of water and spirit." It would be helpful if John explained what "water" and "spirit" mean here, but we can make a good guess. We know from the first chapter about baptism, which is a ritual involving water: *baptizō* is a Greek term meaning "to dip" or "to immerse." And we know that for the followers of Jesus, baptism "in the name of the Father, and of the Son, and of the Holy Spirit" (Matthew 28:19) was an initiation rite. John is likely referring, first, to the water of baptism, but not only this, as we'll see later in this chapter when we meet the Samaritan woman. He is also referring to the Holy Spirit, which some followers understood as being part of the baptismal rite. According to the Synoptic tradition, the Spirit descended on Jesus at his baptism (Matthew 3:16; Mark 1:10; Luke 3:22), and in John 1:32, the Baptizer says about Jesus,

"I saw the Spirit descending like a dove out of heaven, and it remained on him."

I've heard from numerous friends that their baptism was a special moment: they felt cleansed from sin, pristine; as they felt the water on their skin, they felt the palpable presence of the Spirit. Others have mentioned how, when attending the baptism of others, they felt that same special, transcendent moment, when everything was both clear and right. John frequently talks about retrospective thoughts, in which events become clear only with the passing of time. In 12:16, John writes, "His disciples did not understand these things [the immediate antecedent is the Triumphal Entry into Jerusalem] at first, but when Jesus was glorified, then they remembered that these things had been written of him." Reading John 3, with its references to water and spirit, may help people recollect the moments in their lives when confusion gives way to clarity, or, to draw from the Prologue, when chaos yields to order.

While Nicodemus is trying to keep up with what Jesus is saying, Jesus adds to the confusion with another pun. This one works in both Greek and Hebrew. In 3:8, Jesus states—and I'll need to use the Greek again —"The *pneuma* blows where it wills, and you hear the sound of it, but you do not know where it comes from or where it goes. It is the same way with everyone who is born of the *pneuma*." We've already seen this term in the introduction, in the citation to Isaiah 53. The Hebrew term *ruach* (a guttural "ch" as in J. S. Bach) and the Greek *pneuma* can mean "wind" or "breath" or "spirit." Hence the English term "pneumatic," which is an instrument that operates by wind, or the disease pneumonia, which concerns difficulty in breathing. This connection is also, by the way, why churches have organs, which are "wind" instruments: when the organ plays, the wind—or spirit— flows through it to the congregation (if you hear an allusion to Bach here, good).

Our worlds are enriched again. We can feel the Spirit's presence whenever we inhale and exhale, or when a breeze caresses our cheek.

27

Although unlikely in terms of origins, the divine name in Hebrew, often transliterated "Yahweh," can sound like breathing.

John offers one more comment that requires decoding. While some of John's language becomes clearer given knowledge of the Synoptic Gospels, in other cases, such as the "I am" statements or the various terms in the Prologue, such as "beginning," "word," and "light," knowledge of Israel's Scriptures brings both depth and clarity. In John 3:14-15, Jesus tells Nicodemus, "Just as Moses lifted up the snake in the wilderness, so it is necessary that the Son of Humanity be lifted up, that anyone who believes in him/trusts in him may have eternal life." Poor Nicodemus.

The reference to Moses concerns Numbers 21:4-9, a weird account (yes, it is okay to admit that portions of the Bible are weird) in which God initially sends a plague of poisonous snakes to punish the wilderness generation for their complaining: "The soul of the people became discouraged (the Hebrew literally means "short") on the way" (given forty years in the wilderness, I have some sympathy for the complaint). They complain to God and to Moses, "Why have you brought us up from Egypt to die in the wilderness, because there is no bread (i.e., food) and there is no water, and our souls loathe this miserable bread?" I am reminded of an old joke: one customer in the restaurant exclaims, "This food is awful!" to which his dining partner responds, "I know, and the portions are too small."

The people, now dying from snakebite, admit to Moses that they had sinned by complaining and ask him to pray on their behalf. Moses agrees. God relents, but not simply by making the snakes go away (St. Patrick is a long way off). God tells Moses to "make a *seraph*" (yes, as in the *seraphim*, fiery supernatural creatures; most English translations read "poisonous serpent") and put it on a pole. Then, everyone who looks at this image will live. Moses constructs a snake made of bronze, and the image works. According to 2 Kings 18:4, King Hezekiah broke into pieces this bronze serpent, to which the Israelites had been making offerings. Weird.

The technical term for how this serpent works is "apotropaic magic," which means using the symbol of something evil to ward off evil. This is, for example, how gargoyles function.

Now to John: how is the snake Moses lifted up related to the Son of Humanity's being lifted up? Because in John, "lifted up" means both on the cross and to the heavens, above. So too for John, Jesus's crucifixion, a humiliating and painful death, is at the same time his glorification. John 3:15 is, moreover, the first use in the Fourth Gospel of the phrase "eternal life," which for John does not mean "live forever and not die." To the contrary, John takes death very seriously, as the weeping at the tomb of Lazarus in John 11 shows. People die. Lazarus died. Jesus will die. John's point is not simply resurrection to eternal life; by "eternal life" John means much more.

John uses the term "life" (Greek: *zoē*) consistently (if you're bored, you can find all forty verses that use the term, and some of those verses use it more than once). Among them, John 3:16, also to Nicodemus, "For God in this way loved the world that he gave his only Son, so that everyone who believes/has trust in him may not perish but may have eternal life."

Images of the Crucifixion in which Jesus's legs are pulled to the side are meant to suggest a serpentine image. Followers of Jesus who look at a cross, a symbol of death, at the same time see a symbol of life, abundant and eternal. And in this understanding, once again, John has lifted language and imagery from the mundane, to the transcendent.

But our friend Nicodemus, at the end of the chapter and the end of the Gospel, remains in the dark. One of the signs of discipleship in John is an invitation to "come and see," which Jesus addresses to two of John the Baptizer's disciples (John 1:39), and then Nathanael to Philip (1:46), and as will our Samaritan woman to the people in her hometown (4:29). Similarly, Andrew brings his brother Peter to Jesus (1:41-42), and Martha brings Mary to Jesus (11:28). Nicodemus will testify on behalf of Jesus in John 7, and in John 19:39-40, he and Joseph of Arimathea will entomb Jesus with one hundred pounds of myrrh—which is a lot of myrrh—the expectation is that Jesus will remain dead and that his corpse will decay.

The Samaritan Woman

Nicodemus comes to Jesus by night, and he remains in the dark. The Samaritan woman comes at noon, so we readers should know that she is walking in the light and is indeed enlightened. She is known in the many Eastern Orthodox Churches as St. Photini, "the enlightened one"; in Russian, she is also St. Svetlana (the word means the same). Early sermons in the Eastern tradition refer to her as both an "apostle" and an "evangelist," and legends developed that the Emperor Nero, understood to have crucified Peter upside down and beheaded Paul, executed her as well as her sons and her sisters in 64 CE.

Commentators, however, frequently misunderstand this woman. They see her as a five-time loser because she had been married five times and is currently cohabiting with a man to whom she is not married (John 4:18). Then they marvel that Jesus does not condemn her. Missing here is that there may be nothing to condemn. The Synoptic Gospels describe a hypothetical question posed to Jesus by the Sadducees, a group of Jews known, among other things, for not believing in bodily resurrection. Their question: A woman's husband dies. Under the system of Levirate marriage, she is wed to her husband's brother, so that she can bear a son who will inherit the dead husband's name and estate. Brother number two dies, so she marries brother number three, and on through seven brothers. The Sadducees then ask Jesus whose wife she will be in the Resurrection (Matthew 22:28; Mark 12:23; Luke 20:33). My concern here: no one saw her as a "seven-time loser." It is the reader's imagination, not John, who turns the woman into, variously, a gold digger, an impossible wife, or a slut.

Then, commentators suggest she came to the well at "about noon" (John 4:6) because no one else would be there; the other women would go earlier, or later, and not in the noontime heat. She goes alone either because she feels shame in the presence of others, or because everyone else has ostracized her. Then, Jesus once more becomes the hero in that he speaks with her. Wrong again. First, people go to the well when they need water. Second, the noon setting is part of John's extensive light/dark symbolism. Third, the well is "Jacob's well" (John 4:12), and Jacob met his future wife Rachel in "broad daylight" (Genesis 29:7; the Hebrew literally means "the big day"). One of John's points is that Jesus is "greater than our ancestor Jacob" (John 4:12).

Finally, had the woman been, as they say, of "ill repute," there is no reason for the people of Sychar, her village, to leave their city and go to see Jesus simply because she told them, "Come and see" (John 4:29-30). Indeed, by having her say "come and see," John connects the woman to Andrew (1:39), to Philip (1:46), and to the people at Lazarus's tomb (11:34). There may also be a connection to Psalm 66:5, "Come and see the work of God: he is awesome in deeds among the children of Adam [i.e., among mortals]."

Let's grant that the woman is respectable and intelligent, and then hear again her conversation with Jesus. We can now recognize how, as with Nicodemus, Jesus uses words to move her from the earthly to the transcendent, and how, unlike Nicodemus, she keeps up. From this very long chapter, we'll take three soundings.

Give me to drink. (John 4:7)

John 4:4 states that as Jesus was leaving Judea and heading back to Galilee, "It was necessary that he go through Samaria." In terms of navigation, the statement is not true. While going through Samaria is the direct route to Galilee, one could make the journey by going through the Jordan Valley. Since there were tensions between Jews and Samaritans, going by the alternative route from Galilee to Jerusalem was the safer option. The necessity is a theological, not geographical, one. Jesus stops in the city of Sychar, a location otherwise unknown, which John 4:5 identifies as near the land that the patriarch Jacob gave to his son Joseph (see Joshua 24:32).

It being about noon, and Jesus being tired (he is fully human; like the rest of us, he gets tired), he sits by a well. While Nicodemus deliberately came to Jesus, a Samaritan woman, having no idea he would be at the well, comes to draw water. Jesus engages her with the abrupt command, "Give me to drink" (John 4:7). The scene immediately evokes John 2, where there is a lack of wine and Jesus's mother indirectly requests that he do something about it. "What to me and to you, woman?" he asks. Here *he* is the one in need of something to drink. In John 2, off stage, Jesus commands the catering manager to fill six stone jars with water. Now, it is the woman who is the one capable of providing water.

The scene should also remind biblically literate readers of other times where men and women meet at wells, with marriage being the result. In Genesis 24, Abraham's servant meets Rebekah, the future wife of the patriarch Isaac, Abraham's son, at a well. In Genesis 29, Jacob meets Rachel at a well. In Exodus 2, Moses meets his future wife Zipporah at a well. We literate readers, especially if we are thinking literally, will anticipate that Jesus will meet a wife at the well. Here is the problem with thinking literally rather than metaphorically.

Jesus commands a drink. We do not know, however, if he really wants one. If he does, he does not receive it, as the woman never provides him water from the well. Instead, the request is less for liquid than it is the occasion for a discussion, a lesson, about "living water." But we are not there yet.

The woman asks Jesus why he, a Jew, would ask a Samaritan for water, since as John explains, Jews and Samaritans do not have dealings with each other (John 4:9). The text is a paradox, since by their conversation, a Jew and a Samaritan *are* sharing. By being in Samaria, Jesus the Jew is sharing. The disciples, who have gone off to buy lunch, are sharing with other Samaritans. Thus, John sets up this dichotomy only to break it down.

What the Jews and Samaritans do *not* share is the same geographical focus. While Jews understand the Torah as locating the "place that the Lord your God will choose as a dwelling for his name, [where] you shall bring all that I have commanded you: your burnt offerings and your sacrifices, your tithes, and the contributions from your hands, and all your choice vows that you vow to the Lord" (Deuteronomy 12:11) as Mount Zion in Jerusalem, the Samaritans see that place as Mount Gerizim in Samaria.

On this division, Jesus tells the Samaritan woman, "You worship what you do not know; we worship what we know, because salvation is from the Jews" (John 4:22). But this theological difference does not preclude conversation, or fellowship. Jesus does not water down (pardon the water puns, but they flow so easily) his own tradition for the sake of pluralism. Differences can be maintained, strongly, and at the same time friendship can flower.

Jesus asks for a drink, but that is not in fact what he wants. He wants to start a conversation with the woman. I am here reminded of the great rabbi and theologian Abraham Joshua Heschel, who spoke of how God is in search of each one of us. With all the works on humanity's search for God, with all the people who see themselves as "seekers," it's often salutary to flip the script and think about God in search of us, and as wanting to be in relationship with us.

John alludes to Jesus's request in 19:28, where Jesus, as he is being crucified, states, "I thirst." He is, again, not actually thirsty, for John explains that he said this "in order to fulfill the Scripture" (the reference is to Psalm 69:21b in English translations and 69:22 in the Hebrew, "for my thirst they caused me to drink vinegar"). Symbolically, Jesus is thirsty not for sour wine, but for both communion with his followers and for returning to God the Father. Theological desires can be visceral, incarnate, and so Jesus, and we as well, use the language of food, and so of hunger and thirst, to talk about personal need. Thus, John helps us to determine both the object of our thirst, and what will quench it.

I wonder how our lives would change if with each glass of water or cup of coffee, we thought about people who thirst, or Jesus who thirsts. Every swallow becomes a blessing. When that occurs, we are feeling the effects not of caffeine, but of living water.

Living Water

Jesus continues to use enigmatic comments designed to reveal who he is and what he offers. He answers the woman, "If you knew the gift of God, and who it is that is saying to you, 'Give me to drink,' you would have asked him, and he would have given you living water" (John 4:10). Okay then. If someone at a restaurant had said this to me, I would have asked for a different table.

First, it turns out that the woman comes to know this "gift of God," because she will ask Jesus for his living water. Jesus is leading her to what she already knows but does not fully realize. Second, she also eventually realizes who Jesus is, a point Nicodemus never reaches. It just takes her a while to come to full understanding. The same point holds for the man born blind in John 9, for revelation need not come all at once; it can proceed in steps, and so it can grow. Third, she will have to decode "living water," which functions along the same lines as being born *anōthen*, the wind/breath/spirit, and being "lifted up."

The expression "living water" (Hebrew: *mayim chayyim*; Greek: *hydōr* [like hydraulics] *zaō* [same root as *zoē*, "life"]) can also mean "running water," as from a stream or an aqueduct. For example, Genesis 26:19, the Bible's first use of the term, speaks of finding a "well of living water" (translations usually offer "spring water"). The Sychar well would have this same type of water, as from an underground spring. In discussing ritual purity Numbers 19:17 provides one ritual regarding regaining ritual purity following coming in contact with a corpse: "running water" is to be combined with the ashes of the purification sacrifice. Deuteronomy 21:4 mentions a "wadi with running water."

But there is more to this "running water" than just, well, water. Jeremiah 2:13 speaks of God with the same expression: in God's voice, he laments that the people "have forsaken me, the *spring of living water*, and have dug for themselves cisterns, broken cisterns that are not able to hold water." Jeremiah 17:13 uses the same metaphor, "the spring of living water, the Lord." Running water is living water, and living water is God. Jesus is with God and is God; he is by the water, and at the same time he is the water.

As with wind, so with water: when it is mundane and when something much more? The water in a water fountain (bubbler, cooler—language marks where you are from) is different from a water in a font or a *miqveh* (Jewish ritual bath), but if we were simply presented with three glasses of water from these different sites, we could not tell the difference. Origins matter. More, what was once running water can become living water or for that matter, wine.

Two more iterations before we move on. First, John 1 is about John the Baptizer, who baptizes with water. John 2 presents Jesus as turning water into wine at Cana. Water changes its nature, from solid (ice) to liquid to gas. And we change it, from ordinary water to baptismal water to, in some churches, holy water. Jesus (along with several magicians) changes water into wine, and earlier Moses, in Egypt, changes water into blood. And these connections are just, well, a drop in the bucket (a two-pointer for those of you counting puns). That colorless, tasteless liquid is so much more.

Buckets and Wells and Springs

Just as the language of food, of bread and water and wine, can have theological meaning, so can the language of sexuality. At this point, several of my friends get a tad nervous: "AJ," they say, "talking about theological language is all well [as it were] and good, but talking about sex...is this necessary?" My friends put up with a lot. More, sexual imagery and sexual relations can be entirely chaste.

The ancient world was not as squeamish about sexual language as some of us are today. Indeed, in both Jewish and Christian sources, the language of sexuality lent itself easily to theological discourse, since the language of sexuality implies what good theology should be: intimate, involving the body as well as the mind, something that makes our skin tingle and our hearts beat faster.... This connection between theological and sexual language is in part why the language of Jesus as bridegroom is so potent. The Song of Songs (also known as the Song of Solomon or Canticles) is love poetry: for the Jewish tradition, it is the love song between God and Israel. For the Catholic tradition, the love song is between the Christ and the Church, and for many Protestants, the love song exists between the Christ and the soul.

In John 4, sexual banter abounds.

Following Jesus's comment about living water, the woman addresses him with the title, "*Kyrie*"—another double entendre. The term is the Greek translation of the Hebrew YHWH, as noted in the introduction, so it can mean "Lord." It also means "Sir." Is the woman making a theological claim, or just being polite? When does the meaning change?

Here is one of several places where it helps to read John over and over again. When we get to the end of the Gospel, John has made his case for Jesus as Lord. A retrospective reading shows that the woman has in fact gotten the right title, "Lord," and not simply "Sir," even if she does not realize the point yet. John frequently depicts people as making comments that are more profound than they themselves realize. Another example is Caiaphas's statement in 11:50, where he affirms regarding the plot to have Jesus executed lest he and his followers provoke the Romans to attack Jerusalem, "It is better for you that one person (*anthrōpos*) die for the people than to have the whole nation (*ethnos*) destroyed."

Back to the conversation. The woman continues, "You have no bucket, and the well is deep. Where therefore do you have the living/running water?" (4:11). On the mundane level, she is correct: she is the one with the bucket. On the transcendent level, Jesus doesn't need the bucket; he doesn't need to drop the bucket down the well to get running water since he *is* the living water.

However, and here's where people sometimes get nervous: on the sexual level, "wells," "fountains," and "springs" can have additional connotations. Song of Songs 4:12-15 describes a young woman as a "locked garden" and a "sealed spring" (i.e., she is still a virgin), a "garden spring" and a "well of living/running water." Offering good advice, Proverbs 5:15-18 tells young men, "Drink water from your own cistern and a stream from your own well . . . let your spring be blessed and rejoice in the wife of your youth."

I think Jesus had a sense of humor, and John I am sure, based on my study of the Gospel's rhetoric, had no problem drawing on the popular culture of his time to make his case. Some stories in the Gospel are repurposing of accounts in Genesis, Exodus, and 1 Samuel. Some draw on the conventions of Hellenistic rhetoric, some evoke legends of Dionysus the Greek god of wine, and some I think follow the idea of gods as sexual beings—here, as in all other cases, only to explode the category. Thus, given that gods in the broader non-Jewish culture are sexual beings, the idea of a woman flirting with this strange fellow, who seems to be more than human although she cannot quite tell how, makes sense. There's a hint of the god Dionysus in this story as there was in the story of turning water into wine at Cana, but Jesus will prove himself not only more powerful, but more worthy of following. Jesus in John 4 will play along with the literary convention of the language of flirtation, until he demonstrates that while he is a sensual being, he is not going to be husband number six.

Before Jesus has a chance to respond to the comment about the bucket, the woman continues by evoking what Jews and Samaritans share. The chapter will continue to challenge, even explode, the opening comment about Jews not sharing anything with Samaritans. She asks him, "You're not greater than our ancestor Jacob, who gave us this well?" Then she adds, "he himself drank from it and his sons and his flocks" (John 4:12). Her ancestor Jacob is also Jesus's ancestor Jacob, the grandson of Abraham, whose name was changed to "Israel." The Samaritans and Jews share an ancestor.

The Samaritan Woman and Nathanael

In chapter 1, Jesus encounters Philip and exhorts, "Follow me" (John 1:43). Philip finds Nathanael and announces that Jesus is the one whose coming Moses and the prophets predicted, this fellow, "Jesus, son of Joseph, from Nazareth" (1:45). Nathanael asks him, "Can anything good come out of Nazareth?" (1:46). This is a dreadful question, since it manifests geographical prejudice. But just when we may be tempted to condemn Nathanael for his parochialism, it turns out—although we do not know this until John 21:2, that Nathanael is "from Cana in Galilee"! Who knew? He's also from Galilee. What sounded initially bigoted was an in-house joke. Of course, thinks Nathanael, good things come from Galilee.

Then Philip repeats Jesus's words to him, "Come and see" (John 1:46). John's Gospel repeats the motif of one person evangelizing another. Philip invites Nathanael, and in chapter 4, the Samaritan woman will invite the other residents of the village of Sychar in effect to "come and see."

This earlier passage in John has three additional connections to John 4. First, when Jesus sees Nathanael, he announces, "Here is [or, for people who prefer the more biblical expression, 'Behold'] truly an Israelite in whom there is no deceit" (1:47). The comment on the surface is just as parochial as Nathanael's comment about Galilee.

It is tantamount to saying, "Here's a person from Paris, or Moscow, or wherever, who is honest." But Jesus is also joking, since he too is an Israelite, which is another term both for Jews and by extension for Samaritans.

Second, in John 1:48, Nathanael queries Jesus, "Where did you get to know me?" (in other words, how do you know that I am not deceitful?). Jesus responds, "Before Philip called you I saw you under the fig tree" (1:48). From this Nathanael concludes, "Rabbi, you are the Son of God! You are the king of Israel" (1:49). The response floors me. It sets a remarkably low bar for determining messianic identity. It's tantamount to saying, "I saw you getting coffee," or "I saw you in the grocery store." Jesus, I think with a smile, says to him, "Do you believe because I said to you that I saw you under the fig tree? You will see greater things than these" (1:50). I should hope so, if messianic identity is at stake. Nathanael draws an astounding although for John entirely correct conclusion from a limited set of data.

I have the same impression of the Samaritan woman, whose words echo those of Jesus and Philip. She says to the people in Sychar, "Come and see"—right, "come and see." What are they to see? She explains, "A person who said to me everything that I have done. He cannot be the Christ, can he?" (John 4:29). Knowing one's marital history is also not, to me, a particularly high bar for a messianic sign. Turning water into wine is good; feeding five thousand with limited resources is even better; raising the dead is spectacular. But seeing someone under a tree? Knowing someone's marital history? What is meaningful to one person may not be to the next. So "come and see" *for yourself*. . . . And the villagers do so.

Philip and Nathanael, the Samaritan woman and her village, come to regard Jesus as the Messiah not because of signs and wonders (spectacular though they are), but because of their personal encounter with him. John will reinforce this point at the end of the Gospel, when Jesus has a chat with "doubting" Thomas. Jesus says to Thomas, "Because you have seen me you believed (the statement can also be read as a question: "Do you believe because you have seen me?"). Blessed are those who have not seen and yet believe" (John 20:29). Signs can be faked, misinterpreted, or even the acts of the devil. The real proof, if proof there can be, of the presence of God is in what John Wesley called the "heart strangely warmed." You know because you know.

As for the fig tree where Jesus saw Nathanael, a few sermons I have read state that the fig tree represents the place where rabbis teach. Such a comment is comparable to the similar claim that Jesus sat down in the boat when he taught the crowds, because rabbis sit when they teach. Rabbis—by which these sermons are referring to the rabbis of the rabbinic tradition, who lived close to a century after Jesus—don't look for fig trees on which they would hang signs saying "rabbi is in." Rabbis, at least according to rabbinic sources, which date to about 170 years after the crucifixion of Jesus, teach anywhere people will listen. They've got no particular focus on fig trees, or mulberry bushes, or mustard plants. As far as sitting down in the boat, Jesus sat down because that's the safer way to be in a boat, comments on walking on water notwithstanding.

I'd like to think that John mentioned the fig tree because that is where Jesus saw Nathanael. Not every place needs to have an allegorical significance. On the other hand, John makes the point that any place can be a place of revelation. So too for the well where Jesus meets the Samaritan woman. Yes, the well reminds us of those various "meet at the well" scenes from the Scriptures of Israel. It is also a place where people go, comparable to the knitting store or the coffee shop. Again, any site can be the location of revelation; any site can be a place of evangelism.

Third, Jesus tells Nathanael, "You will see heaven opened and the angels of God ascending and descending upon the Son of Humanity" (John 1:51). This line is an allusion to Genesis 28:12, the famous scene of "Jacob's ladder." John's symbolism is at work here, for just as that ladder was the link between heaven and earth, so for John, Jesus is that link, that mediator, between heaven and earth, between the human and the divine.

The reference does more: the allusion here to Jacob, for the biblically literate reader, prepares us for John 4, which takes place—wait for it—at *Jacob's well*. Not only does each verse in John's Gospel reflect upon other verses but also the entire text reflects upon the Scriptures of Israel and brings new meaning to them. Each time we read John's Gospel, we should find something new, and each time we read John in light (the metaphor is deliberate) of the Scriptures of Israel, we should see something new, or clearer, in both older texts and in John.

A few final notes about this well. First, there is no notice in the Scriptures of Israel of Jacob purchasing a well or of his giving it to his children. Second, that lack of evidence does not matter to the author of John's Gospel, who is the first to mention it in literature. The Samaritan community may well have recognized the well years, or centuries, before John wrote. Thus, the well raises the question of whose history we read, a very good question.

Next, the well has been a Christian pilgrimage site since the fourth century, with various churches constructed around it over the years. The well is today located in the (Greek Orthodox) Church of St. Photini by the city of Nablus in what is today called the West Bank. Like the Pool of Beth-Zatha John mentions in chapter 5, it is a real place. With all the symbolism John offers, underneath remains a real well, with real water, in a location with its own history.

Back to the Well

The Samaritan woman had asked Jesus if he is greater than "our father Jacob," the father Samaritans share with Jews. The answer is, for John, yes (I am tempted to say "duh," as in "Of course, did you miss the first three chapters?"). Jesus then tells her that the well water cannot do what he can do. To drink basic "running water" is fine, but after a while, thirst again kicks in. Then he moves to theological proclamation: "Whoever might drink of the water I will give them will never be thirsty." Why? "The water that I will give them will become in them a spring of water gushing up (the term has the connotation of leaping or jumping) to eternal life" (4:14). Wells and buckets and fountains and springs gushing up, OH MY!

It takes a while to process these comments. Water is suddenly not just water, with or without electrolytes. It is not just "running water" from the well, or the faucet, but "living water." The thirst that it quenches is not just a parched throat, but a spiritual desire. At the same time, every glass of water or coffee or lemonade or something stronger can be a moment of spiritual realization. John is brilliant here. Every breath you take, every cake you bake...every swallow can be a moment of revelation when we realize how our body works, how taste works, and it can be a moment of revelation.

Christians of all denominations participate in a fellowship meal, an *agape* meal, Eucharist or Communion, the Lord's Supper, and so on. The presence of Jesus in these rituals is palpable. How wonderful it would be if Christians, when they eat the bread (gluten free is available in many churches) or drink the wine (or, if we must, grape juice) were to have a sense of eternal life in the taste, the swallowing. It's beautiful.

The Samaritan woman, whether sarcastically or flirtatiously, says, "Sir (again, *kyrie*, which also means "Lord"), give me this water so that I may never thirst or have to keep passing through here to draw water" (4:15). Good for her. She has turned the tables (faucets) on Jesus. He said, "Give me to drink," and now she's telling him, "Give me..." If God can be in search of us, then we too can make requests.

"I see you are a prophet." (John 4:19)

Jesus knows the woman is flirting, and that's not the direction in which he wishes to continue. He changes the subject by commanding her, "Go, call your husband, and come back here" (4:16). She spoke of never having to return to the well; he insists that she go and return. This seemingly odd comment works in terms of John's theology. Possessing living water, being in the Spirit, does not replace the mundane aspects of life, just as being born anew does not mean that one can avoid death. Jesus is suggesting that she will come back to the well, many times, but now with, well, a better spring in her step.

The woman responds that she has no husband, and Jesus confirms her comment: true, she is presently not married, but she had been married five times, and now she is living with a man who is not her husband (John 4:18). From his notice about her five marriages and her current living arrangements, the woman concludes, generously, I think, that Jesus is a "prophet" (4:19). The comment is odd, since prophets typically make statements about the future, not the past, and the statements they make are typically open-ended: repent and return to righteousness or bad things will happen.

Jesus takes the cue from the Samaritan woman and then offers a prophecy: he tells her, "The hour is coming when neither on this mountain nor in Jerusalem will you worship the Father... the hour is coming and is now here, when the true worshipers will worship the Father in spirit [Spirit?] and truth [Truth]" (4:21, 23a). At this point, what we thought we knew falls apart. First, in speaking of the "Father" Jesus shows again that Jews and Samaritans share much in common, including the acknowledgment of the same God. Second, time has collapsed: the hour both is and is not here, when this worship takes place: this collapse is created by the presence of Jesus, who is for the Gospel eternal, and who represents (and is) God. As the Book of Revelation puts it, God is the one "who was and is and is to come" (1:8; 4:8). The words *spirit* and *truth* can refer to attitudes, but since Jesus also embodies the Holy Spirit and since he is filled with truth (1:14), brings truth (1:17), is called the truth (5:33), and self-identifies as "the Truth" (14:6), the reference to "truth" here becomes more than an attitude. It becomes a relationship with Jesus.

The Jewish followers of Jesus and quite possibly the Gentile ones as well continued to worship in the Jerusalem Temple until it was destroyed by the Romans in 70 CE. They worshipped in house churches, and eventually in freestanding buildings. They do so to this day. Jews then and now worshipped in the Temple and in synagogues and in homes and in the outdoors and wherever they were. Since God is omnipresent, worship should also take place anywhere and everywhere. John reinforces the point with this sense of the omnipresence of the divine, who can be met anywhere: at a wedding, at a well, at a tomb, anywhere. Again, the Gospel gives a palpable sense of divinity.

I am. (John 4:26)

The woman accepts Jesus's comments and moves to another future statement: she insists that she knows the Christ is coming, "and when that one comes, he will announce to us all things" (4:25). Jesus responds, at least in most English translations, "I am he, the one who is speaking to you." However, the Greek reads, literally, *egō eimi*, "I am," the words Moses heard from the burning bush (Exodus 3:14, Septuagint). This is the first of the Gospel's "I am" statements. Others include "I am the bread of life" (6:35, 48), "I am the light of the world" (8:12; 9:5); "I am the good shepherd" (10:11, 14); "I am the resurrection and the life" (11:25); "I am the way and the truth and the life" (14:6); and "I am the true vine" (15:1). Moreover, in John 8:58, Jesus says, "Before Abraham was, I am," and in 18:5, he identifies himself to the soldiers who come to arrest him as "I am," words powerful enough to make the soldiers fall down.

The "I am statements" show us again the power of words, and here of metaphor and of poetry. No words can fully express divinity, but images of bread and vine, light and shepherd, help us see different facets of the omnifaceted divine presence. The title "I am" or in Hebrew, "I will be what I will be," necessarily holds multiple meanings. The Greek "I am" is essential and permanent; the Hebrew is open, and what we might call existential. God is all this and more. And it is the Samaritan woman who is the first after Moses to hear this name revealed directly.

The Samaritan woman leaves her water jug by the well and runs to tell the people in Sychar that she thinks she has encountered the Messiah. Like a true disciple, she announces, "Come and see" (4:29) and brings the people to Jesus. John 4:39 tells us that "from that city many Samaritans believed in him because of the word (*logos*) of the woman who bore witness (*martyreō*, hence the English, "martyr") 'He said to me all that I have done.'" Like Nathanael who proclaims Jesus the Messiah because of his seeing the potential disciple under the tree, the rationale for the woman and the townspeople—Jesus stating the woman's marital history—is not a great messianic sign. But we readers know that Jesus will do many more striking signs.

The story ends when the Samaritans say to the woman that they believe "no longer because of what you said" but because they have heard Jesus themselves (4:42). For a number of years, I very much disliked this ending. I wanted the woman to be praised for being the first successful evangelist. As I've gotten older, however, I've come to appreciate this comment. The woman does what a good teacher should do: get out of the way and let the students draw their own conclusions. I have an image of her returning to her home, as the sun is setting; she closes her eyes and experiences a new type of light. She feels the breeze and senses the spirit. She takes a sip of cold water, and she feels it course through her body, making every part of her feel more alive.

On Food, a Final Thought

When the disciples return, they urge Jesus, "Rabbi, eat" (4:31). I relate to this line: when I would come home from elementary school, my grandmother, who lived with us, would say, "Eat something" (although she never called me "rabbi"). The disciples missed the move from "Give me to drink" to the conversation about "living water." Jesus speaks to them in the same enigmatic way he addressed both Nicodemus and the Samarian, "I have food to eat that you do not know" (4:32).

Had I been one of the disciples, shopping for food, worrying about what Jesus would like to eat, haggling about the price, and then schlepping back to the well, only to be told that he has food that I did not know about, I suspect I would be a tad miffed. John does not tell us that the disciples were annoyed (they likely had more patience than I do), but 4:33 does note that the disciples asked one another if anyone had brought Jesus something to eat.

The passage looks to me like a Johannine version of an account in Matthew and Mark where after Jesus feeds over five thousand people on one occasion and then over four thousand on another occasion, Jesus warns his disciples to beware of the "yeast of the Pharisees and the yeast of Herod" (Mark 8:15) or in Matthew's version, "The yeast of the Pharisees and Sadducees" (Matthew 16:6). The disciples, who have difficulty recognizing a metaphor, conclude that Jesus is upset because they had forgotten to bring bread. Jesus, who has no trouble providing lunch, then takes several verses to excoriate the disciples on listening with better ears. In John's version, their listening is not quite so half-baked.

Jesus replies to his disciples in John 4:34, "My food is that I might do the will of the One who sent me, and to complete his work." As the woman understands the transition from running water used to quench physical thirst to living water for spiritual sustenance, the disciples need to move from thinking of a sandwich to thinking of salvation.

Spirit and breath and wind, being born again and being born from above or anew, running water and living water, wells and springs and fountains, physical food and spiritual food . . . the third and fourth chapters of John continue the process of sacralizing the mundane, of changing our language and so, if we can keep up with Jesus, changing our perspective.

CHAPTER 3

The Healing of the Man at the Pool

(John 5)

The man born blind in John 9, the subject of our next chapter, is a favorite of many sermons because he models the appropriate response to Jesus. Receiving the gift of sight, he seeks to know more about the stranger who healed him; he stands up to the Pharisees, whom John depicts as antagonistic to Jesus. Like the Samaritan woman, he starts by recognizing Jesus as a prophet and then develops his new (in)sight to a higher Christology. He anticipates the new family Jesus creates in the man's separation from his cowardly parents; he issues a "come and see" moment, albeit facetiously, when he says to Jesus's opponents, "Do you also want to become his disciples?" (9:27); he receives, like the Samaritan woman, Jesus's direct statement of his identity, "The one speaking with you is he [the Son of Humanity] (9:37). Finally, he worships Jesus (9:38). What's not to like?

On the other hand, the fellow at the pool strikes many, including me, as petulant. He appears to be a sinner, and although he reports to "the Jews" that Jesus had healed his paralysis (5:15), the result is not the gaining of more followers but the increase in persecution.

The Samaritan woman sets the model for the man born blind in chapter 9: both receive revelation from Jesus about his identity, both develop in their understanding. To some extent Nicodemus sets the model for the paralyzed man in chapter 5. Nicodemus never quite gets the call, and the paralyzed man never comes to faith.

In this chapter we visit with the paralyzed man at the pool of Beth Zatha (also known as Bethesda, or Bethsaida) to determine what his problem is and why it might continue (John 5:1-16). In this case as well as John 9, we also raise the question of how to talk about disability and healing in the Bible, given that the language of disability is often used for disparaging individuals.

Location, Location, Location (John 5:1-4)

In the Synoptic Gospels, Jesus heals a paralyzed individual who is let down through the roof of a house by his friends. The occasion, as Mark 2:5 notes, has Jesus noticing the faith of the helpers and then saying to the fellow on the bed, "Child, your sins are forgiven." After an expected kerfuffle about who has the authority to forgive sins, Jesus orders the fellow, "Take up your bed and go to your house" (see Matthew 9:6; Mark 2:11; Luke 5:24). While it is possible that Jesus walked around Galilee and Judea telling people to "take up your bed and walk," I find it just as likely that John knew the comment and built another story around it. The accounts have the same outline: a paralyzed person, the inability of this person to get to the place of healing (the Synoptic account because the house where Jesus was teaching was too crowded; the Johannine account because of lack of someone to help move the man into the water); the line about the bed; questions of sin; and people who criticize the healing. By looking at John's version of the story, we find new insights concerning such matters as the relationship of feasting and healing, the competition among the disabled for health care, learned helplessness, and the very problematic connection sometimes drawn between disability and sin.

Our account begins with John 5:1, the notice that there was "a festival [the Greek can also mean "feast"] of the Jews, and Jesus went up to Jerusalem." Unlike Mark and Matthew, which depict Jesus only going to Jerusalem during the Passover festival, which will be the last week of his life, John presents Jesus as going back and forth from Jerusalem to Galilee. Luke locates Jesus in Jerusalem in his infancy, where Simeon and Anna encounter him, and then again when Jesus is twelve years old, where he interacts with teachers in the Temple. John's itinerary strikes me more historically plausible: Jesus may well have gone to Jerusalem on multiple occasions to celebrate the festivals at the Temple with his fellow Jews.

John does not tell us what this particular festival was. There are three pilgrimage festivals: Passover, celebrating the Exodus from enslavement in Egypt; Shavuot, the feast of weeks, celebrating the giving of the Torah on Mount Sinai (the Greek term for this festival is Pentecost, or "fifty," since it take place seven weeks plus one day after the Exodus); and Sukkot or Tabernacles or Booths, commemorating the time the children of Israel were in the wilderness. Since John 7:2 mentions this third festival, perhaps that was the one intended. I'm relatively certain that if we knew the specific holiday, monographs would be written to explain its symbolism in relation to the healing.

Pilgrimage festivals were not the only reason people went to the Temple. Jews would go for other occasions, whether to celebrate a birth or a good harvest, to pray in the Temple as one might make a special trip to pray in a particular church or synagogue, to celebrate other holidays, as Jesus does when he goes to the Temple for the "Feast of Dedication," also known as Hannukah, the holiday commemorating the rededication of the Temple following its desecration by the Syrian king Antiochus IV Epiphanes (John 10:22). It was a place for celebration and lament, for meeting other Jews from various places in Judea and Galilee and from the Diaspora. It was even a place where Gentiles went, whether to pray to the Jewish God or because the magnificent Temple complex was in part a tourist attraction.

Although John does not give the details, the notice of the "festival" deserves comment. Too often I find that church programs, with few exceptions, are not celebratory (and yes, I spend a lot of time in churches, now increasingly so since the end of Covid restrictions). The doors to the sanctuary close on Sunday morning at 11:00; the children are hushed or led out of the main sanctuary following "children's church" or "event for all ages," or whatever that special moment where kids come up to the front of the church and hear a story; people stifle coughs, and yawns, and the serious work of worship commences. Perhaps matters might be different if, with the exception of explicitly serious times, such as Lent, or Holy Week, there might be more festivity in the worship.

The term "festival" also sets up the questions of who "celebrates" and how best can one celebrate if one cannot participate in all the activities. The question of disability is present before we meet the cast of characters.

John next details the location: "In Jerusalem, by the 'ovine,' there is a pool, called in Hebrew Beth-Zatha, which has five colonnades" (5:2). On the awkward translation: most English translations have the scene set "by the Sheep Gate"; the Greek does not mention a gate. The Greek term *probatikos*, which I have translated "ovine," means "having to do with sheep." The addition of "Gate" likely comes from the notice in Nehemiah 3:1 of the construction of one of the gates to the Temple area. Colonnades, also called porticoes, are columns positioned at strategic locations in order to support a roof.

As far as the location goes, there are multiple occasions when I ask (I really do, I ask, usually out loud) the evangelists why they include certain details. Why mention that Nathanael was under a fig tree? Why mention the five porticoes? Rarely do the evangelists answer, and I've not found commentaries to be much help. It may be that the fig tree gets mentioned in John 1 because that is in fact where Jesus saw Nathanael. Perhaps John mentions the five porticoes to give a sense of "you are there" to the readers: John is describing a big place.

The name of the place, Beth-zatha, is not Hebrew but Aramaic, a cognate language (like French is to Italian or Spanish is to Portuguese). Beth (better, "bet," without the *h*-sound), as in Bethlehem or Bethsaida, means "house." The "Zatha" part is a problem. Some manuscripts offer "Bethsaida" and others "Bethesda," a term that fits the Copper Scroll, one of the scrolls associated with other scrolls found by the Dead Sea.

Josephus mentions six times in his multivolumed *Jewish War* a newly built city north of the Jerusalem Temple called Bezetha, which he translates as "New City." Or, if the name, from the Aramaic, were Beth-hesda, then it means something like "house of grace" or "house of divine steadfastness" (readers may be familiar with the Hebrew cognate *chesed*). This would be an appropriate name for a place known for healing. John 5:3 confirms the concern for healing by noting that in the colonnades "were lying many who were weak: blind, unable to walk, withered [lit. dried; the implication is atrophied arms and/ or legs]." Then again, the name may come from Beth-esda, "house of flowing [water]."

Side note on translations: the term I have translated "withered," Greek *xēros*, means to dry up. The same word describes the "withered hand" of the man whom Jesus heals in the Capernaum synagogue in Matthew 12, Mark 3, and Luke 6, and a cognate refers to what Jesus does to the woman suffering hemorrhaging: he dries her up (Mark 5:29). Next, the Greek word for writing is *graphō* (whence the English "graphite" and "graphology"). When *xēros* and *graphō* are combined, the expression can mean "dry writing": hence, with a bit of adjustment, the combination gets us the name "xerox." Copy that!

Like Jacob's well, we know the location where this healing takes place. The site, excavated in the 1880s, is in Jerusalem's Muslim Quarter, near the Church of Saint Anne. The pool is rectangular, with colonnades on all four sides as well as another on a wall that bisects the pool. Hence, a pool with five colonnades. The site has been used for millennia for healing, with various gods being invoked. From the second century of the common era (i.e., after Jesus) are the archaeological remains of an asklepion, a temple named after Greek god of healing, Asclepius, where people would seek healing and, through dreams, a diagnosis and plan of treatment.

The location is comparable to modern hot baths or natural spas. We can do more: given that Jews engaged in bathing for purposes of regaining ritual purity in *miqva'ot*, we might also speculate that this pool also functioned as a *miqveh*. And that would mean—again, wait for it—that the pool had "running water," the same expression we encountered in John 4 regarding "living water."

John the evangelist has a very good, detailed sense of Jerusalem's geography, and his literary alter ego, the "Beloved Disciple," has contacts in the high priest's house. This knowledge of the city is one of the reasons biblical scholars think that the author of the Gospel is not the Galilean fisherman, John the son of Zebedee; the author or at least the authority that provided many of the details of the Gospel, is more likely a well-connected Jerusalem-based disciple.

The Missing Verse, John 5:4

John 5:4 is a verse missing from most Bibles (go ahead, check your text). John 5:4 picks up from 5:3 about the numerous people with various disabilities. It states that they were "waiting for the stirring of the water, for an angel of the Lord went down at appropriate times (*kata kairon*) into the pool and stirred up (lit. "troubled") the water. Therefore, the first one who after the stirring of the water was made well from whatever diseases that person had." The reasons for its absence are that the verse is missing from some of the major early manuscripts and that the sentence has a higher number than would be expected of words absent from the rest of the Gospels. Many scholars regard it as a later addition (the technical term is "interpolation") and so not part of John's original manuscript or at least not part of the earliest versions we have.

I agree: I doubt this verse was an original piece of the Gospel. I also find its content disturbing ("troubling"): it suggests numerous suffering individuals attempting to win the healing lottery by pushing others out of their way to get to the pool first. The image makes the angel a sadist and the people in competition. Good thing the verse is omitted in many modern printings. It is there primarily to explain why the man who eventually will meet Jesus had been there, on one translation of the Greek, for thirty-eight years (John 5:5). Don't worry: we'll get to him shortly.

On the other much more positive hand, I do like the idea of stirring up the waters, and so of running water. This phenomenon regarding the angel appears in the works of ancient Christian authors such as the Bordeaux pilgrim in the early fourth century. Finally, this verse provided the inspiration for the spiritual, "Wade in the Water" with the refrain, "God's gonna trouble the water." The spiritual understands the fuller impact of the Gospel's language: when Jesus states that "the truth (Truth) will make you free" (John 8:32), the meaning of freedom was, for those escaping slavery, not just a metaphor.

And there was some person there who had been weak for thirty-eight years. (John 5:5)

Thirty-eight years is a long time, and it would seem even longer to those who are "weak" or "sick" (the Greek term has both connotations). Scholars have debated the symbolic value of thirty-eight years, especially since the number is used occasionally in the Scriptures of Israel to talk about what happened in the thirty-eighth year of the reign of king so and so (see, e.g., 1 Kings 16:29; 2 Kings 15:8).

The best intertext for our verse, already mentioned by the church father Cyril of Alexandria (early fifth century) is probably Deuteronomy 2:14, which notes that it took the Israelites who escaped slavery in Egypt thirty-eight years to get from Kardesh-barnea to the Wadi Zered, "until the entire generation of warriors had died" as God had planned. Thirty-eight years thus can function as an approximation of the passing of a generation (the typical count for a generation is forty years); in Deuteronomy it can also indicate the time for one ethos, that of enslavement and the battles to counter its effects, to be replaced by another, that of freedom and the concerns for what one can do now and in the future. I have the strong impression that the original authors of "Wade in the Water" also made this connection.

People who excel in math might be inclined to note that two prime numbers, 2 and 19, when multiplied, yield 38: Or, better, 38 is what we get when we square the first three prime numbers (2x2)+ (3x3)+(5x5). For those of you who like mathematics (I am not a fellow traveler), the multiplication of prime numbers finds a match in the writings of St. Augustine (who apparently did like math); Augustine noted that the 153 fish mentioned in John 21:11 equals the sum of the first seventeen numbers (1+2+3...).

Whatever the symbolic implications of the number, the fellow is not doing well, and as the number indicates, he has not been doing well for a long time.

"Do you want to be made healthy?" (John 5:6)

When Jesus sees the fellow, he realizes that he had been there for a long time (I picture, anachronistically, old calendars with dates marked off, old newspapers, and a candy wrapper from 4 BCE), he asks him, "Do you want to be made healthy (the Greek term is *hygiēs*, whence "hygiene")?" (John 5:6). I admit that my initial thought on reading this verse was "Not a great question." On second thought, I've concluded that it is a profound question. Not everyone who is ailing wants to be made well. Identity can become so caught up in the sense of infirmity, especially if coupled with appreciation of sympathy and the willingness of others to help, that the status quo becomes the more comfortable position. Physicians have greater success rates when their patients want to be healed. Not everyone does.

Complaining, Kvetching, Lamenting

The man does not answer directly. Technically, he engages a rhetorical form sometimes called indirect discourse. Instead of directly asking for something, he makes a statement to which most people would understand the point. We saw this construction in the comment Jesus's mother makes to him, "They have no wine." The statement is not just a notice of the obvious; it is an oblique plea for help.

Our fellow speaks to a situation of helplessness designed to evoke pity, "Sir [*kyrie*, "lord"], I have no person to put me into the pool when the water is stirred up, and when I am coming, another goes down before me" (John 5:7). I wonder: Did he ever ask for help? Or did he spend his days bemoaning his condition rather than doing what he could to help others?

On the other hand, perhaps the fellow is exhausted. For years he asked for help and received none. For years he sought healings, from miracle-working rabbis, temples dedicated to Asclepius, doctors, and magicians. Nothing worked. Perhaps he has given up. And yet, he is still alive, which means that someone has provided him food, and helped him with cleaning up after basic bodily functions. Perhaps he leaves the pool in the evening to return to a home where there are people to help him. It's very easy to judge when we don't have all the details.

Jesus says to him, "Rise, take your mat, and walk around." (John 5:8)

The business about taking the mat, which we also saw with the paralyzed fellow let down through the roof in the Synoptic accounts, initially seemed odd to me. For a person unable to walk for thirty-eight years to stand up is impressive enough; the bed business seems like overkill. Yes, it can indicate renewed upper body strength, and it can suggest a nice reversal in that the person comes in carried on a bed and leaves carrying the bed. A friend suggested, when I mentioned this oddity, that perhaps Jesus was concerned that others might trip over the mat. Could be. John puts the reference here as a clue to readers: the mat will later become part of the story. Don't dismiss minor details. Everything can have meaning.

Compared to the Synoptic Gospels, John's individual stories tend to be longer, with one genre, here a "healing narrative," segueing into another genre, here a "controversy story" about how best to remember the Sabbath and keep it holy (so Exodus 20:8). The man does as Jesus commanded: he rises, picks up his bed, and walks around (John 5:9a). At this point, I would have expected the man to praise Jesus, or at the very least say "thank you." If he were less obtuse, he might have asked Jesus questions, as did Nicodemus and the Samaritan woman at the well. I would have started, after the profusion of gratitude, with a "who are you?" (My mother would have insisted that I also get an address so I could send a handwritten thank-you note.) From this fellow at the pool, nothing.

And that day was a Sabbath. (John 5:9b)

Jews, and even many Christians, have been debating how best to keep the Sabbath as a day of rest, how to determine what constitutes work, and so on. At the time of Jesus, there was no formal code indicating what counted as "work" and what did not, and different groups had, and to this day still have, various customs regarding Sabbath observance.

From the Synoptic tradition, the major concern is whether healing on the Sabbath would be considered a violation. The Synoptic story of the man with the "dried up" hand epitomizes the genre: Jesus goes into a synagogue, sees the man with the unusable hand, commands him to stretch out his hand, and "his hand was healed" (passive voice; Mark 3:5; Luke 6:10). The healing is accomplished by command, not by action; the passive—sometimes called the "divine passive"—is a grammatical way of suggesting that God performed the healing. Jesus is guilty of nothing. He did not concoct a medication; he did not perform an operation. Rather, he helps those whom he has healed more fully celebrate the Sabbath. Nor is there any law insisting, "Thou shalt not heal on the Sabbath."

John turns the tables on the genre by depicting the man, not Jesus, being accused of violation of Sabbath custom, "Therefore, the Jews were saying to the man who had been healed, 'It is the sabbath, and it is not permitted for you to carry your mat'" (John 5:10). The issue should be less fraught than the Synoptic healings: there's a big difference between restoring a person to physical wholeness and carrying a mat. Healing for Jesus is a theological necessity; carrying a mat, not so much.

John 5:10 raises numerous questions, including whether the man knew it was the Sabbath (likely), knew that carrying a mat was a problem (perhaps), disregards Sabbath practice given that after thirty-eight years, he's feeling pretty good and doesn't care what day it is (possible).

On the cultural front, the issue of what one is permitted to carry on the Sabbath does occupy biblical texts, rabbinic literature, and is a concern for Orthodox Jews to this day. Jeremiah 17:21-22 advises the covenant community, "Keep watch (or take care), for the sake of your souls (Hebrew: *nefesh*, with the sense of "your lives"), that you do not lift up a load on the Sabbath day, or bring it into the gates of Jerusalem, and do not bring out a load from your houses on the Sabbath day or do any work, but you shall make holy (i.e., sanctify) the Sabbath day, just as I commanded your ancestors."

Rabbinic law proscribes carrying items outside the home; however, the rabbis, like the Pharisees before them, sought to make Torah easier to follow. From this concern comes the *eruv* (from the Hebrew for "blending"), the idea of making all the households in a neighborhood into a single household, so that on the Sabbath, for example, carrying things, and even people, is permitted. Nashville, where I live, has an *eruv*, and this makes it possible for members of my (Orthodox) synagogue to carry on the Sabbath, whether bringing food to a neighbor or pushing a baby in a stroller to the synagogue and back home.

The idea of not carrying I find to be helpful: it helps me to think about what I need to bring, how big a purse I need, or a suitcase. Today I rarely go anywhere without the cell phone, but it wasn't all that long ago that no one had a cell phone. When I was a child, I would watch the TV show *Get Smart*, with the famous (or at least it was then) shoe phone. What do we need, what can we leave behind, what should we leave behind?

Back to our John 5. I am annoyed at the fellow who complains and then fails to thank Jesus; I'm distressed by the Jews, the term John uses seventy-odd times, with the majority of uses being derogatory, who tell him what is and is not permitted rather than celebrate that thirty-eight years of weakness have ended. For John, the "Jews" designates the people opposed to Jesus and aligned with the world. In John 5, the evangelist wants to show their heartlessness. They express not delight for the healing, but disgust for the action.

More, I'm concerned about Jesus, who—given that John portrays him as having foresight—would have anticipated that the "Jews'" would challenge the man. Jesus had not only raised him up, he has set him up. On a psychological level, I am not a fan of this approach. I do not want people deliberately being "led into temptation" or "brought to the test," especially when they are not expecting it.

The fellow had numerous options for a response, from "I did not know it was the Sabbath" to "Where is it written that carrying a mat is forbidden," to "Perhaps instead you might note that after thirty-eight years, I'm walking." Given John's motif of one person bringing another to Jesus, his best response should have been, "Come and see...who made me healthy." Nope. Instead, he attempts to shift responsibility, "He answered them, 'The one who made me healthy, that one said to me, 'Take up your mat and walk around'" (John 5:11).

John continues, "They asked him, "Who is the person who said to you, 'Take it up and walk around?'" (John 5:12). The man should have asked this question. Not only does he fail to ask Jesus who he is, the man has no clue. John explains, "And the one who had made healthy did not know who he was, for Jesus has left without being noticed by (or even left because of) the crowd in that place" (John 5:13). At this point, the man should go in search of Jesus. He fails. Jesus must find him. At this point as well, the "Jews" have no one to challenge, so any concern over the Sabbath should have dissipated. It does not, and it does not because of our now-healed but still annoying (yes, I'm being uncharitable) guy carrying his mat.

After these things, Jesus found him in the Temple and said to him, "Look, you have become healthy. Do not sin any more, so that nothing worse happens to you." (John 5:14)

Wow. So much going on in this verse. First, Jesus finds the fellow. My initial thought was that this would be relatively easy, for despite the Temple being an enormous structure, not that many folks would be carrying around a mat. Second, the text gives no indication that the man attempted to find Jesus. That strikes me as bizarre. Given that Jesus has already performed several signs, including those John does not recount, and knowing the Synoptic tradition where crowds continue to follow Jesus in search of a healing, it's likely other people were also seeking him. Third, the Temple is the perfect place to give thanks for a healing: we do not see the man at prayer or giving thanks.

Then comes Jesus's comment, "Do not sin any more." The comment suggests that the reason for the man's thirty-eight-year illness was because of sin, and such coupling of sin and disability is a problem both historically and pastorally. Historically, Jews did not typically couple the two. Isaac is blind, but from old age not sin (Genesis 27:1); Jonathan's son cannot walk well, but because of a childhood accident, not sin (2 Samuel 4:4). Infertility is a disability in that it is a condition in which the body is unable to do what is culturally expected and often personally very much wanted. We'll come back to the question of linking sin to disability when we meet the man born blind in chapter 9; here, we simply note that unless

59

someone like Jesus states that disability is a punishment for, or the result of, sin, we should not make the link.

That link confirms that there was something problematic about the man. Whereas in the Synoptic account of the fellow let down through the roof, Jesus says, "your sins are forgiven you," there is nothing here about forgiving the man. Nor has the man asked for forgiveness or even acknowledged his sin. The details remain between Jesus and him.

Finally, Jesus warns that something worse may happen were the man to sin. He had already been sick for thirty-eight years; it's hard to imagine something worse, but we do so anyway. My suspicion is that the line is less about additional physical suffering and more about eternal damnation. In John's Gospel, which tends to have a binary view of either damned or saved, the man can make a choice. The man has been healed, and warned. And he apparently doesn't care.

For John, the ultimate sin is failing to believe in Jesus. And yet, this is not something the man can control, any more than can our friend Nicodemus. Either one believes, or one does not. As I've noted in multiple occasions, belief is more like love than Sudoku—it is a matter of the heart, not the intellect. For me, what is important is what can be controlled, and on this count the man fails both my moral compass and my sense of etiquette. He makes no statement of gratitude; he offers no confession of his previous sin; he does not even ask Jesus who he is! What a dolt (okay, that was uncharitable, but this fellow really does annoy me).

Instead, he "went away and announced to the Jews that it was Jesus who made him healthy" (John 5:15). Really, this is the best he can do? He likely knew that the "Jews," who accused him of violating Sabbath protocols, would not be in favor of the man who told him to pick up his mat. He had to have known that he was setting Jesus up. This is not a "come to Jesus" moment; it's a "go get Jesus" plot. How dare he!

Rather than acknowledge his sin, and rather than offer prayers of thanksgiving—both of which suggest personal weakness or lack—he deflects. If Jesus is arrested, he doesn't have to give thanks, and he doesn't have to worry about his own guilt being brought up. Further, now that he can walk, he no longer can demand pity or attention. He has to begin a new life on his own. Whether he has the emotional strength to do so, or whether he would prefer to be back on his mat, will remain not just open questions, but also warnings.

The man gets what he wanted, deflection: "On account of this [that is, the fellow's testimony], the Jews were persecuting Jesus, because he was doing these things on the Sabbath" (John 5:16). The Gospel tradition frequently depicts Jesus and his fellow Jews in discussion over Sabbath observance. The impression Christians frequently get from these discussions is that the Sabbath was a burden, not a blessing. This would be the wrong impression. But our concern for this chapter is not the particulars of observing a day of rest; it is the end of the story of the man who received a healing. He issues no thanks, he sets Jesus up, he fails to come to his defense, and we are left with the impression that his thirty-eight years of disability were caused by his sin. It's a terrible picture.

John 3:16 famously says that "God so loved the world...." If God can manage, perhaps I can find a bit more generosity. But I still wonder about all those other people waiting by the pool: what might they be thinking? And for those who still need freedom from whatever is holding them back, when will the waters be troubled?

CHAPTER 4

The Man Born Blind

(John 9)

Being in the Dark

From the first chapter, the Gospel of John plays on distinctions between light and dark. The Prologue tells us that Jesus is the light that shines in the darkness, and that darkness cannot overtake that light. In 3:19, Jesus tells Nicodemus, "The light has come into the world, and people loved the darkness rather than light for their deeds were evil" (in my less generous moments, I give a nod to the fellow from John 5). In John 12:46, Jesus announces that he has "come as light into the world." Thus, when John records a chapter about a man healed of blindness, the import of the chapter is necessarily about not only physical healing, but also spiritual enlightenment.

Sometimes, given how metaphors work, as light is associated with enlightenment, so the dark and its attendant images—blackness, blindness, dim bulbs, and so on—are associated with ignorance. Metaphors can be dangerous: they can inculcate prejudice or preclude inclusivity and value. Once we see (see, the visual metaphor—it's pervasive) the problem, we realize that we are conditioned to view darkness with some sense of fear or negativity. But we can do better. Light requires dark because the spectrum is not a dualism. Thus, I want to put in a few good words about darkness and, by extension, a recognition that those who cannot see may have other sensory gifts and talents.

While the Gospels connect the idea of physical blindness with moral dimness or lack of enlightenment, the metaphor shows the privilege, and the ignorance, of sighted people. Matthew 15:14 (cf. Luke 6:39) gives us the metaphor of "blind guides of the blind," with the saying, "if one blind person guides another, both will fall into a pit." No, they will not. People who are blind have, since antiquity, worked out ways of avoiding pitfalls. In the Jewish tradition, they are among God's beloved, from Isaac and Eli the priest in 1 Samuel 3:2 to Job who attests to his righteousness by speaking of his care for the blind and those unable to walk (Job 29:15). The Psalms praise God who "opens the eyes of the blind "(Psalm 146:8) as does Isaiah (35:5; 42:7, 16), and Jeremiah 31:8 includes the blind as well as those who cannot walk and "those pregnant and in labor"—that is, people who may have difficulty traveling—among those in exile who will be gathered back to the national Jewish homeland.

We have discussed how John's Prologue reflects and refracts the book of Genesis, which begins (as it were) with darkness covering the face of the deep, and a mighty wind/wind from God/Spirit of God sweeping over or hovering over the face of the deep waters. Light has not yet been created, but on one reading of Genesis, the Spirit is already present. The Spirit is not antithetical to darkness but can be found within it. And there are lessons from this verse, lessons about the beauty of darkness as well as light.

We cannot, at least in our human bodies, walk fully in the light. Indeed, we are just as sightless in total darkness as we are in the brightest light. Complete darkness and complete light are both obscure. We also know that to go from total darkness into bright light, or from bright light into a darkened room, our eyes need time to adjust. Moreover, to see the glories of the light—such as the stars in the heavens—we need the darkness. Increasing numbers of locations suffer from "light pollution," such that some cities are requiring a dimming of lights in the evening so that people can once again see the stars.

Nor, to extend the metaphor, can we shine brightly all the time—it's too exhausting. We'll burn out unless we take the time to recharge.

The dark is also the time of revelation. It is at midnight when Jesus makes his statement to Nicodemus about being born from above. While Nicodemus doesn't quite get the point, we readers do. It is in the dark where the fetus forms. It is in the dark where the seed germinates. As Exodus 20:21 states, "Moses drew near to the thick darkness where God was."

Deuteronomy 5:22-23 again finds God in the darkness, as Moses proclaims: "These words the Lord spoke to your assembly at the mountain, from the midst of the fire, the cloud, and the thick darkness, with a great voice. . . . When you heard the voice from the midst of the darkness, and the mountain was burning with fire, you approached me." In 1 Kings 8:12, Solomon pronounces, "The Lord has said that he would dwell in thick darkness"—and this thick darkness becomes the holy of holies, the inner sanctum in the Temple.

For those inclined to mysticism, it is in the dark night of the soul that we grow to spiritual maturity. In the dark, we are at our most vulnerable, and so most honest.

And it is in the darkness when most of us rest—when we close our eyes. This is the time we should be refueling. If we do not rest, we cannot work; if we do not embrace the darkness, and the rest it provides us, we can neither walk in the light nor be in the light. Sometimes we must turn the light off—the lamp beneath which we write our lectures or work out our budgets; the computer light that occupies us with countless tasks. Turn them off, close our eyes, and rest. The world does rotate: let someone else do the walking in the light while we lie down. And once we are restored, we are better prepared to walk in the light. The Gospels give us numerous examples of what taking this path means.

In John 9:1, Jesus sees a man; the man cannot see him in return. I'm struck by this notice. It suggests that even when we cannot see, or perceive, we are seen and known. The point is not the paranoid sense of Big Brother, or Santa Claus, who sees you when you're sleeping, and so on. It is the sense of palpable love and guidance. Jesus sees the man, just as he "saw [the paralyzed man] lying there" (John 5:6). The setup is the same: Jesus sees someone in need of a healing. In this variation on the theme, the reader waits to see how the scene plays out.

As he walked along, he saw a person blind from birth. (John 9:1)

Again, John presents a healing. Jesus sees the disabled individual; the disability has lasted a long time (thirty-eight years, or in this case, since birth); the healing has a connection to a pool, there is a question of Jesus's identity, the topic of sin is broached, the healing takes place on the Sabbath. But in this case the fellow who receives his sight becomes a disciple rather than a traitor. That the healing concerns blindness, and that in the previous chapter Jesus announced that he is the "light of the world" (John 8:12), a point John repeats in 9:5, is our first clue that the story will go in a different direction.

His disciples asked him, "Rabbi, who sinned, this one or his parents, that he was born blind?" (John 9:2)

The question presumes that sin causes disability, which—unless the text hints at this issue, as it does with the fellow in chapter 5 (a scene in which the disciples are absent)—would not be the case. The disciples' question needs to be corrected. I would have been happier here had Jesus sat the fellows down and given them a lesson on disability.

First, he would have stated that the sins of the parents are *not* visited upon the children. While Exodus 34:7 speaks of bringing punishment for the sin of the parents upon the children, and the children's children, to the third and fourth generation, Ezekiel 18:20 puts a stop to this idea: "A child shall not carry the sin of a parent, and a parent shall not carry the sin of a child." As the King James Version puts it, "The son shall not bear the iniquity of the father, neither shall the father bear the iniquity of the son." Similarly, before Ezekiel, Jeremiah spoke of the day when "they will not still say, 'the parents ate sour grapes, and the children's teeth are blunted.' For all will die for their own sins; everyone who eats sour grapes, that person's teeth shall be blunted" (Jeremiah 31:29-30; this is the same chapter that describes the "new covenant" to be written on people's hearts).

Second, he would have noted the oddity of someone sinning prenatally. While there was some sense of reincarnation floating around at the time—a point Mark 6:14 and Matthew 14:2 may also suggest in depicting Herod Antipas as wondering if Jesus were John the Baptizer "raised from the dead."

Third, Jesus would have decoupled sin and disability by mentioning that God takes special care of the blind, and therefore so should anyone who follows Torah. It is God who, for God's own reasons, causes people to be "seeing or blind" (Exodus 4:11). And it is God who insists, "You shall not curse a deaf person or put a stumbling block before a blind person" (Leviticus 19:14), indeed, "Cursed be the one who causes a blind person on the road to go astray" (Deuteronomy 27:18).

Finally, Jesus would have recollected with the disciples his conversation with Nicodemus, with its concern for being born anew or born from above. If people are "born in darkness" and then they encounter Jesus, the light of the world, John hints that they can expect a type of rebirth. Being "born" in the Fourth Gospel has multiple meanings.

John, in typical dualistic manner whereby one is either saved or damned, team-Jesus or team-Satan, develops the narrative of the man who was blind by twice more referring to sin. In 9:24, the "Jews" call to the man who now sees and command him, "Give glory to God. We know that this person (i.e., Jesus) is a sinner." The irony is that by praising Jesus, the man who now sees *is* giving glory to God (see John 1:1, "the Word was God"). More, by calling Jesus a sinner, the Jews condemn themselves. In 9:34, the opponents charge the man born blind, "You were born entirely in sins, and you are teaching us?" The answer for John is "Yes, of course I am trying to teach you, but you will not listen."

"So that may be revealed God's works in him." (John 9:3)

The verse reminds me of John 11:4, where Jesus explains to his disciples that Lazarus's illness and subsequent death is "for God's glory." I wonder if this man, like the fellow by the pool, had spent thirty-eight years waiting for the ability to see. My friends, however, inform me that I am being uncharitable. In their view (another visual metaphor), the blind man's happiness upon seeing for the first time in his life was worth the wait; more, he provided the occasion for others to give glory to God.

The setting appears still to be Jerusalem, where Jesus had gone to celebrate the Festival of Sukkot, also called Tabernacles or Booths. The ceremony in the Temple included pouring of a water libation, so we might expect water imagery. More, the holiday, one of the three pilgrimage festivals, was associated with great joy. Thus, if we have a story set on Sukkot that concerns a person born blind, we can expect a healing, something to do with water, and great joy. We shall not be disappointed.

The Pool of Siloam

Following Jesus's christological statements about being the light of the world in 9:4-5, John 9:6 explains, laconically, "Having said these things, he spat on the ground and made mud out of the spit and anointed with the mud the man's eyes." While saliva (human and dog) was considered to have medical benefits (I am reminded of the famous parental cure of "kissing a boo-boo"), Jesus's action comes without any announcement. Jesus says nothing to the man at all. Did the man hear Jesus's comments about being the light of the world? Did he reach out with his hands or call out with his voice? Was he hoping for a coin or two, since we learn in John 9:8 that he was a beggar, only to find himself with mud on his eyes?

The account should remind us of Mark 8:23-25, where in Bethsaida, Jesus encounters a blind man: Jesus leads him out of the city, puts spittle on his eyes, and asks him what he sees. The man responds that he sees people, but they look like walking trees (I am reminded of Tolkien's Ents from *Lord of the Rings*). Jesus again puts his hands on the man's eyes, and now his sight is 20/20. Because he knows what people and trees look like, he would not have been blind from birth. John repeats the basic idea of a slowly growing enlightenment, but ramps up the miracle with the greater severity of the disability.

We might also be reminded of Mark 7:33, where Jesus heals a man who can neither hear nor speak when he put "his fingers into his ears, and he spitting, he touched his tongue." The visceral images of spit and mud and touching may have suggested medicinal practices to ancient readers; I appreciate the "touch" aspects, of body to body. Jesus is not here prescribing from a distance; he is literally "hands on."

The scene gets even weirder. Both blind and now finding his eyes caked with mud, the fellow receives Jesus's instruction in 9:7a, "Go, wash in the pool of Siloam" (which, John tell us, is interpreted as meaning "Sent"). And the fellow finds his way. John says nothing about anyone leading the man to the pool: he is not helpless; he is not lost.

As he goes, perhaps he is thinking of a story he had heard from the Jewish tradition, about how Elisha the prophet sent Naaman, a Syrian general suffering from a skin disease, to immerse himself in the Jordan River (2 Kings 5:10-14) in order to be healed. He might be thinking of the origins of this pool at the end of the waterway King Hezekiah constructed so that Jerusalem would have better access to water when the Assyrian king Sennacherib attempted to conquer Judea (see 2 Kings 18:13) in the late 1700s BCE. The pool suggests healing and rescue and miracle and good planning.

John tells us that Siloam means "sent"—the Greek is the same word that gives us the term "apostle." Perhaps the fellow thought that the person who made the mud from his spit was sent from God.

Earlier in the Gospel, Jesus self-identifies with this term, as in John 3:17, "God did not *send* the Son into the world in order to condemn the world, but so that the world might be saved through him" (there are several other "sent" references reflecting Christology—while the formerly blind man does not know these references, we readers do).

Or perhaps he is thinking that the pool, a *miqveh*, would symbolize a new life for him. He is not ritually impure since blindness does not cause impurity, but the feel of that "living water" might be restorative. John's early Christian readers may have thought of baptism and so of new life. Perhaps he is thinking of the Festival of Sukkot, where water was drawn from this very pool (the details are explained in Mishnah *Sukkot*) and then poured on the altar, with—wait for it—Jesus's own body being a type of altar where the divine can be encountered. John had already hinted at this water ceremony in 7:37, where "on the last day of the festival, the great day" Jesus cries out, "Let anyone who is thirsty come to me and drink." The connection to Jesus's conversation with the Samaritan woman will, like the story of the paralyzed man in John 5, provide John 9 one of its numerous intertexts.

Or again, maybe the fellow is thinking about the mud. The original human being was created from the earth, from *adamah*, arable soil (hence the name "adam"), so perhaps he thought about Adam and creation, or the beginnings of new world for him. Perhaps he thought about the healing properties of nature, of dirt. Or perhaps he is thinking of the spit from Jesus's own mouth, and Jesus's own fingers.

For archaeologists, the pool of Siloam is indicative of how, after close to two millennia, places mentioned in the Bible (the pool already appears in Isaiah 8:6; the Hebrew text calls the pool *Shiloach*; the Septuagint reads *Silōam*) can be located. The problem, however, is that archaeologists disagree as to exactly where this pool is, and there are two major pools in contention. I am not an archaeologist (I cannot imagine—on my knees, in the dirt and dust, I'd break a nail—I don't even like gardening), but I am both grateful for what they do and aware that archaeological finds, like literary texts, require inter-pretation, which are always subject to change.

The end of John 9:7 states that "he went and washed and he came back seeing." He came back, not like the fellow with the mat. He sees, but given John's heavy use of metaphor, he has yet to achieve full enlightenment.

Therefore, the neighbors and those who had seen him at first as a beggar were saying, "Isn't this one the one who was sitting and begging?" (John 9:8)

They had "seen" him, which is already a good start, given how easy it is to overlook those who sit and beg, or who distribute newspapers for supporting the homeless, or who stand with signs asking for work.

Contrary to several sermons and commentaries on this text, the fellow is not an "outcast"—he has a social role. Beggars in antiquity had and, to this day in various places in the world, have a place in society. The same point holds for Mark 10:46, which locates a blind man known as Bartimaeus on the road to Jericho. To contribute to their care is a form of piety. To those who insist that the role of beggar is a humiliating one, that perspective comes from a position of privilege. Luke 16:3, part of the parable of the dishonest CFO, depicts the man saying to himself, "I am ashamed to beg." He cannot imagine himself doing what countless people have done, generation after generation. People do what they can with the resources that they have.

The neighbors, to use the English expression, cannot believe their eyes. When we see someone in a different setting, we must adjust our perception and our knowledge. The man is twice changed: no longer sitting, he now stands; no longer begging, he now has more to contribute than providing others the opportunity of following Torah or showing generosity. He can contribute by testifying to Jesus.

While "some were saying, 'It is he,' others were saying, 'no, but it is someone like him. He was saying, 'I am'" (John 9:9). The verse is brilliant. As people debated who Jesus is, with some saying he is the Messiah and others insisting that the Messiah cannot come from Galilee (John 7:41), so now people debate the identity of the formerly blind man. The debate returns to Christology in John 9:16, with some of the Pharisees insisting that Jesus cannot be from God because he works on the Sabbath, while others insisting that a person who sins cannot perform such signs.

Next, the man identifies himself with the Greek words "I am" (*egō eimi*), the Greek Old Testament's translation of the Tetragrammaton (YHWH), and Jesus's own self-identification, the beginning of all the "I am" statements. The man is clearly not Jesus, but he witnesses to him. In 9:4, Jesus tells his disciples, "We must work the works of him who sent me," and here the fellow who had been blind continues that work in his witness. Finally, the bystanders—perhaps better, onlookers—ask him, "How were your eyes opened?" (John 9:10).

The person called Jesus. (9:11)

Somehow, the man knows who provided the healing, whether by intuition, or overhearing, or John's condensing of the narrative. However he knows, he knows. He stands in contrast to the fellow with the mat. He names the one who healed him, succinctly describes the process—"Jesus made mud, anointed my eyes, and said to me, 'Go to Siloam and wash,"—explains his compliance with "I went therefore and washing," and confirms the healing, "I received sight" (John 9:11). The sentence is not only an efficient summary, it's also a perfect missionary pitch.

When the onlookers then ask, "Where is that one?" the man replies, "I do not know" (9:12). Here is John's motif of Jesus's absent presence (yes, I know this is an oxymoron; bear with me). People in the Gospel frequently question where Jesus is to be found. In 7:34 (see also 7:36), Jesus explains, "You will seek me, but you will not find me; and where I am, you are not able to come." He repeats the point in 13:33, "You will seek me...where I am going, you are not able to come." But Jesus can be found whenever there is light in the darkness, wherever his followers bear good fruit in his name, wherever a breeze can be felt, or water can quench a thirst. The man's affirmation occurs apart from Jesus's own presence; the man, able to see, represents Jesus's ability to heal, and in particular his role as "light of the world."

The disciples, together with the Paraclete, the "Holy Spirit," represent Jesus in the world, and the formerly blind man has already identified himself with the phrase *egō eimi*, "I am," so John now depicts the man as being placed in the position Jesus frequently occupies, that of being tested by opponents.

They brought to the Pharisees the one who had formerly been blind. (John 9:13)

The scene reverses the typical move where people bring others to Jesus, where they "come and see" and find their savior. Now people bring the formerly blind man to the Pharisees. Ironically, he will witness to them, but they do not accept. And suddenly—although given the shift from a healing narrative to a Sabbath controversy in chapter 5 we should not be surprised—John tells us, "It was the Sabbath day when Jesus made the mud and opened his eyes" (John 9:14). The healing becomes another Sabbath controversy.

Carrying a mat, which was not necessary, violates the concept of Sabbath rest. In John 9, for Jesus the healing was necessary, since the light of the world has to bring light. There is no law saying, "Thou shalt not heal on the Sabbath"; there was also no reason for Jesus to spit on the ground, turn dirt into mud, and spread the glop onto the man's eyes. He could have commanded the man's eyes to be open, as he arranged the water to turn to wine, or as he facilitated from a distance the second sign, the healing of the official's son (John 4:46-54). Thus, the issue with the mud is deliberately provocative, as was the issue with the mat.

The provocation provides Jesus's interlocutors the chance to ask more questions, and in the answers to tease out additional matters of Christology. The Pharisees, after debating whether Jesus is or is not from God—they omit the possibility that Jesus is on team-Satan—they ask the healed man what he thinks about the fellow who opened his eyes. The Pharisees do not doubt that Jesus performed the miracle. Their concern is the date, not the miracle itself. The man does not speak to the question of what is permitted on the Sabbath. Rather, he makes a christological point, "He is a prophet" (John 9:17).

The Samaritan woman called Jesus a prophet because he knew about her marital history. The formerly blind man calls Jesus a prophet because, like Elisha, he facilitated his healing from a disability. Both the Samaritan woman and the formerly blind man need to move to the next step, for in the Gospels, Jesus is more than a prophet. The man also has more to lose than the Samaritan woman: while her evangelism is well received by the people in Sychar who then invite Jesus to stay with them, the once-blind man is interrogated and, by the end of the chapter, expelled from his own community. The expulsion works for the narrative, but it is probably literary license on John's part, since we have no evidence of first-century synagogues expelling Jesus-followers. For John, proclaiming the Gospel can both unite and divide; the same point holds true today.

It was the Sabbath. (John 9:14)

Only now do we learn that the day Jesus healed the man by making mud and anointing his eyes was also the Sabbath. We have another iteration of John 5, the Sabbath healing by the pool. But whereas in the earlier chapter the concern was carrying a mat, here the concern has greater christological import: the issue is not a person carrying a mat, but Jesus himself who made the mud.

The setting looks like a trial, but it is not a formal one, since trials could not be held on the Sabbath. Nevertheless, the Pharisees interrogate the man, and unlike the fellow in chapter 9, the now-seeing man speaks the truth: when the Pharisees ask him how he obtained the healing, the man bluntly states, "He put mud on my eyes. And I washed. And I see" (9:15).

Following their internal debate about whether a sinner can restore sight (it is a good question), the opponents (now called "the Jews") speak to the man's parents. Wondering if the healing were rigged, they ask the parents, "Is this one your son, who you say was born blind?" (9:19). The parents give the right answer: Yes, this is our son. Yes, he was born blind. Perhaps they continued to support him; perhaps by his begging he was able to support them. But then they punt since they fear being "put out of the synagogue" (Greek: *aposynagōgos*, a term John invents). As noted, we have no early evidence of Jews expelling fellow Jews who proclaimed Jesus to be Lord; plus, all synagogues were independent.

Claims that John is presenting in this narrative a history of his "community" as if John offers a two-stage play, one set in the late 20s and early 30s, the time of Jesus, and the other in the 90s, the time John writes, at best overstate. The Gospels are narratives addressed to any follower of Jesus. John, who likely had access to the Synoptic Gospels, is writing also for followers who knew the other stories. Finally, the negative comments about the synagogue serve primarily as a warning to readers: stay away from these places! The language is rhetorical not historical, and it is part of John's broader agenda to distinguish Jesus and his followers from "the Jews," an irony given that Jesus and all his initial followers were, in fact, Jews.

Refusing to answer questions about their son, the parents advise these "Jews" to speak directly to him since he is old enough to speak for himself (9:21-23).

Their comments do more than heighten the drama. By opting for fear rather than faith, the formerly blind man's father and mother divorce themselves from the role of parents. Just as the man is "born anew" by having his status changed from born blind to born anew into enlightenment, so he finds a new family distinct from his biological parents. The scene repeats when Jesus, dying on the cross, entrusts to each other his mother and his Beloved Disciple.

Don't you also want to become his disciples? (John 9:27)

The interrogation continues, and the enlightened fellow continues to speak the truth as he understands it. More, he stands up to his accusers. After repeating that he has told them what he knows about Jesus and how the healing occurred, he states, "I have told you already, and you would not listen. Why do you want to hear it again? Don't you also want to become his disciples?" (John 9:27). Great line! The more they question him, the more they provide him the opportunity to testify.

For the purposes of the Gospel, the man emerges as moving from darkness to light, from ignorance to knowledge, and from his own family to the family of Jesus. It is therefore not surprising that at the end of the discussion, the "Jews...cast him out" (the Greek verb in 9:34 is the same term used to describe an exorcism, a "casting out"). It is also not surprising that Jesus, who has been absent during the interrogation, now reappears to provide another lesson in Christology. The man who has gained his sight, like the Samaritan woman, needs to move beyond seeing Jesus as a prophet to seeing him as the light of the world.

Do you believe in the Son of Humanity? (John 9:35)

Jesus begins not with a pronouncement but with his own question: "Do you believe in the Son of Humanity?" The title, which evokes the figure in Daniel 7:13, "one like a son of humanity" (i.e., an angelic being in human form) and which could be translated "child of humanity" or, traditionally, "son of man" (*anthrōpos*) requires definition. The expression can refer to any human being, as with God's address to Ezekiel as "son of humanity." It can also be a messianic indicator.

Like the Samaritan woman, the man then interrogates Jesus. She asked Jesus where she could get the living water; the man asks Jesus, "who is he, *kyrie* (sir, or Lord), say to me, so that I may believe in him" (9:36). Then comes Jesus's self-revelation, "You have seen him"—right, *seen* him, both with your physical eyes and with your spiritual vision. More, "the one speaking with you, that one is" (9:37). The man responds appropriately with both word and action: "*Kyrie*"—here clearly "lord" and not just "sir"—"I believe." John concludes, "And he worshiped him" (9:38).

The chapter ends with reversals. The man who had sat and begged now bends the knee in worship; the one who was blind can now see. Conversely, Jesus explains that he entered "this world for judgment, so that those who do not see may see, and those who do see may become blind" (9:39). When the Pharisees, recognizing his critique, question him, he condemns them: "Now that you say that 'we see,' your sin remains" (9:41).

My preference is that everyone comes away with sight, defined variously. The Pharisees, whom John associates with "the Jews," cannot see since they have not been among those who are called. Faith is no more of a choice than is sight. Faith comes from the heart, not the intellect. Or, from some theological perspectives, faith comes from being called by the divine and not from personal choice. For example, in Galatians 1:15, Paul talks about being "called through [God's] grace." This idea of predestination is also one reading of John 6:44a, "No one is able to come to me unless the Father, the one who sent me, would draw him [or her]." This is why a belief system that makes infinite sense to one person makes no sense to another.

Yet action is a choice. Condemning people for not believing is not a helpful choice; showing love as manifested in action is. Condemning people for questioning is not a helpful choice; belief should not come at the expense of one's rational faculties but should be enhanced by those faculties. Walking in the light is fine; being blinded by it (thank you, Bruce Springsteen) not so much. I wonder what the relationship of this man will be with his parents after Jesus leaves. Will they reconcile? Will the son disown his parents and the parents their son?

How lovely it would be if belief could bring people together rather than pull them apart.

Finally, according to Isaiah 35:5, the time is coming when "the eyes of the blind shall be opened and the ears of the deaf unstopped" (see also Isaiah 29:18; 42:7). For Isaiah the issue is not spiritual lack but physical disability. Perhaps, in the end, as we think about Jesus as light of the world, and his followers as light of the world, we might also think of health care. The spiritual and the physical need not be mutually exclusive.

CHAPTER 5

Foot Washing

(John 12 & 13)

Similar to the Synoptic Gospels, John has an account of a woman who anoints Jesus. For Matthew 26:6-13 and Mark 14:3-9, a woman in Bethany, on the outskirts of Jerusalem, anoints Jesus on his head at the beginning of the Passion Narrative. Someone in Mark and the disciples in Matthew complain about the waste. In Luke 7:36-50, a woman somewhere in Galilee anoints Jesus's feet, bathes his feet with her tears, and then wipes them dry with her hair. The host, Simon the Pharisee, complains in internal monologue about Jesus's allowing a woman "who was a sinner" (Luke 7:39) to provide him this service.

John, who may well have had access to the Synoptic accounts, splits the difference in chapter 12. The setting is the last week in Jerusalem (so Matthew and Mark), and the anointing is of Jesus's feet (so Luke). Our chapter focuses on John's distinct version, including how Mary's anointing anticipates Jesus's washing the disciples' feet in the next chapter.

John adds distinct touches: identifying the anointing woman as Mary the sister of Martha and Lazarus; identifying the one who complains as Judas, with his motive being a concern for pocketing the money rather than giving to the poor. John also draws our senses to attention: the sense of smell, as the scent of the ointment contrasts the stench Martha worries will emerge from Lazarus's tomb in the previous chapter.

In John 13, Jesus will to a great extent repeat Mary's action. At his last supper with his followers, he washes their feet. Again, someone complains, this time Peter, who cannot imagine Jesus would so subordinate himself. And Jesus then provides another lesson on discipleship.

In this chapter, we focus on the service that Mary provides and then Jesus both provides and interprets. Our concerns will also include the senses of smell and touch, the role of the human body, and the questions both of how to provide service without being servile and how to receive service without feeling shame.

From Death to Life to Death

Six days before the Passover Jesus came to Bethany... *(John 12:1a)*

Jesus has been to Jerusalem for the celebration of the Passover, the commemoration of the Israelites' escape from centuries of slavery in Egypt. Jesus, in John's Gospel, embodies and then, for John, replaces the meaning of this and other holidays. For the "Feast of Dedication" (Hannukah), a midwinter celebration marked with light, Jesus is the "light of the world." For Sukkot, the Feast of Tabernacles or Booths, a holiday marked by water libations, Jesus both provides and is "Living Water." For Passover, Jesus—by his death at the times the lambs are slaughtered in the Temple for the Passover meals—becomes a New Passover himself: Jesus is the one who saves his people from the (angel of) death. John even reinterprets the Passover offering by turning it into an offering with respect to sin, since John the Baptizer identified Jesus as "the lamb of God who takes away the sin of the world" (John 1:29).

John sets the scene for Mary's footwashing "six days before the Passover." The temporal marker, like John's noting of the day and the hour, should not be passed over (as it were). Any time a holiday approaches, many of us go into overdrive: buy food, clean, re-clean, buy more food, repeat. Passover is the time when Jews traditionally remove all products containing leaven (e.g., bread) from the home. In Nashville, where I live, we Jews donate the food to the local food bank. We prepare for the seder meal (*seder* is the Hebrew word for "order"; it signals that the meal follows a certain order in terms of what prayers we say, what we eat, when we eat and drink, and so on forth as a Eucharistic celebration or a Communion meal follows a particular order), the home-based celebration of Passover. My husband cooks; I take out the special dishes for Passover (which belonged to my mother's mother), make sure the crystal glasses are clean (they belonged to my husband's aunt Elsie), polish the silver candlesticks (from my mother) and so on to make sure the table also holds memories of relatives no longer with us.

Passover is a time of celebration of freedom from slavery in Egypt; it is a time of hope for universal freedom, safety, and peace. It is a time of making memories and then adding to them, year after year. Families and friends come together, eat and drink, tell stories, sing songs, and say prayers. The youngest person at the table recites the "four questions," each of which begins by asking why this night, this first night of Passover, is different from all other nights. Each seder is the same, and each is different.

The time should be a joyous one. For the people gathered at this meal in John 12, it is particularly joyous, since in the previous chapter, Jesus performed the seventh of the signs John records: a resurrection.

Jesus... came to Bethany, where Lazarus was, whom he had raised from the dead. (John 12:1b)

John likes geographical indicators, whether Nathanael from Cana in Galilee, or the wedding at Cana, or the village of Sychar. Just as wind or water, taste or scent or touch can hold traces of the sacred, so can locations, whether mentioned in the Gospel or experienced in our lives. Mark and Matthew mention Bethany as the location where the woman anointed Jesus's head. Luke adds four verses from the end of the Gospel (24:50), that it was at Bethany where Jesus blesses his apostles and then was carried into the heavens, a moment traditionally called the Ascension.

I admit that John 12:1, the association of Bethany with Lazarus, bothers me a bit. In Luke 10:38-42, the home of Mary and Martha appears to belong to Martha, who is in the role of host. There is no mention of Lazarus their brother in Luke's Gospel, although Luke does have a parable about a fellow named Lazarus (he is the only named person in a parable), who, like the brother of Mary and Martha, also dies and who, the "rich man" in the parable suggests, should return from heaven (he's in the "bosom of Abraham") to tell people on earth to repent (Luke 16:19-31). Whether John turned the parable into a narrative, or the name Lazarus became attached to the parable because of John's narrative, or Jesus named the poor man in the parable Lazarus because he knew of his friend's illness, or some alternative connection, will continue to occupy biblical scholars who worry about such matters.

John enriches the details.

Already in chapter 1, we learn that it was in Bethany where John the Baptizer proclaimed Jesus "the one who is coming after me" and he added, "I am not worthy to untie the strap of his sandal" (John 1:27-28). Reading John 12 in light of John 1, we have questions of service and worth; John's pronouncement of how great Jesus is makes the contrast in chapter 13 more intense, since Jesus will not only untie the straps of his disciples' sandals but also he will then wash their feet.

John next mentions Bethany in chapter 11 where we learn that Lazarus was from Bethany, and that Bethany was also "the village of Mary and Martha her sister" (11:1). This is a striking formulation. John mentions Lazarus first but then connects the village with Mary. Instead of foregrounding Martha, as does Luke, John focuses on Mary. Thus, Bethany must be associated with all three figures, and so it is a place of death and new life, of food and service, a place where both traitors and faithful disciples connect. In John 12:1, Bethany now becomes "where Lazarus was." The city takes on new meaning depending on how it is introduced. When we visit places more than once, which memories come to the fore: the great restaurant, the delayed train, the nursery or the hospice, the home of this person rather than that? Each visit brings new memories, with the older ones shuffled into new locations or painted in different colors.

In 11:18, John tells us, correctly, that Bethany was about two miles (the Greek reads "fifteen stadia"; "two miles" sounds shorter to me) outside of Jerusalem. Since we know Jesus has come to Jerusalem to die, since his hour has come, Bethany provides that one moment of respite before the end. There is still time to turn back. He will not.

And, since we know from John 11, the story of the raising of Lazarus, that the sisters Mary and Martha are also present, we can anticipate what they will do in this setting: Martha, who confessed Jesus to be "Lord . . . you are the Messiah (*Christos*), the Son of God, the one coming into the world" (John 11:27), will continue to treat him both with enormous respect and will continue to show herself to be a good friend. Mary, who came to see Jesus after Martha summoned her, and who also brought with her "many of the Jews" who then came to believe in Jesus (John 11:45) will continue to show her devotion.

We can add one more iteration to the geographical marker. We've already noted that "Beth" (better, "bet") in Hebrew means "house," so that Bethlehem is "house of bread" and Bethsaida is "house of, well, something." Bethany has been understood to mean "house of happiness," "house of answers," "house of figs," and "house of the poor" or even "house of the suffering." The variety of explanations seems to fit the story in John 12, which is an account of joy and suffering, loyalty and betrayal, and questions whose answers only become clear at the end of the Gospel.

There they made a dinner for him. (John 12:2a)

I like the idea of giving a dinner "for Jesus"—the setting is much more focused on him than in the Synoptic accounts where Jesus appears to be one of many invited to dinner. I'm also happy that this setting is not a typical testimonial dinner, which my friend Martin describes as a setting "where everything that needs to be said is said, and where everyone has to say it." I also like the "they"—which means Mary, Martha, and Lazarus but perhaps not only them. The family certainly put together this meal, but perhaps the "they" included others, such as the "Jews" who came to console Mary at her brother's death (John 11:31).

This is not the only dinner the Gospel depicts. Back in John 6, set when "the Passover, the festival of the Jews, was near" (6:4) and so anticipating our dinner in chapter 11, set more or less at the same time but there on a mountain in Galilee, Jesus provides a dinner for "a large crowd" (6:5). Philip anticipates feeding them would require over "two hundred denarii" (6:7; to give a sense of the cost, a denarius was the daily wage for day laborers). Jesus then feeds the five thousand. He leaves the area when the people who had been fed, as did the Samaritan woman in John 4 and the formerly blind man in John 9, perceive him to be a prophet but then seek to "seize him to make him king" (6:15). His hour to be proclaimed king, which is the hour of both his death and his glorification, is not yet. In John 12, there is no hungry crowd or political push. There is no need for Jesus to perform a sign. The time is for him to be with friends. We've already noted that in this Gospel, Jesus is in search of being in relationship with his brothers and sisters; here, at a dinner, he finds what he had been seeking. The time here is for others to give him good gifts.

In John 13, Jesus has his final meal with his disciples. There, he arranges for the dinner. He is host, whether to five thousand or to twelve. He serves, and he allows himself to be served. Both roles, guest and host, are blessed.

Martha served, and Lazarus was one of those at the table with him. (John 12:2b)

As in Luke 10:38-42, Martha again serves, but here her service is not seen as secondary. "Martha served," as do Mary and Lazarus. Martha wanted help with the service. The issue for Martha in Luke 10 is not turning radishes into flowers or folding a napkin. The term "serve" both in Luke 10 and John 12 translates the Greek *diakoneō*, whence the term "deacon." By the time Luke wrote the Gospel, the ecclesial office of "deacon" was already in place; Paul mentions deacons along with bishops as early as Philippians 1:1. In Romans 16:1, Paul references "our sister Phoebe, a deacon of the assembly (*ekklēsia*) at Cenchreae (the port of Corinth). Thus, when I hear that Martha is busy with much "deacon-ing," I think not of upscale dinners but of providing food and care for community members who need it. No wonder in Luke's account she is anxious; no wonder she wants help.

If John had access to Luke's Gospel, which seems to me likely, here John retells the story of the two sisters. Martha is still active, and Mary is still at the feet of Jesus, but now they work, as they did in John 11, together. Harmony is restored to the household.

Lazarus is at a table with Jesus. At some point, I do think Martha and Mary joined him as well. As for whether Lazarus also served, he does even if he is not on his feet. His very presence serves Jesus because his return from the grave testifies to Jesus as "the resurrection and the life" (John 11:25). Sometimes who we are and what we have experienced can be as important as what we do. That presence also assures readers that just as Jesus can call Lazarus from the tomb, so God can do the same for Jesus.

Lazarus's last action in the narrative is to sit at table with Jesus, which strikes me as a great conclusion. Yet it is not the one that will prevail. Following the dinner, in John 12:9, "a great crowd of the Jews" came to Bethany not only because of Jesus "but also to see

Lazarus, whom he had raised from the dead." Again, John offers a "come and see" moment with eyes trained not only on Jesus but also on Lazarus, whose body testifies to what Jesus can do. The problem is that, according to the next verse, "The chief priests also planned to kill Lazarus " (12:10). Not only is Jesus a political danger, in chapter 6 the people's candidate for king, but so is Lazarus since he represents the power Jesus has. We are known by the company we keep. To be with Jesus is to have eternal life; it is also to risk rejection, even martyrdom.

Lazarus's last reference in the Gospel is in 12:17, where John reports that the crowds who saw Lazarus called out from the tomb testify to what Jesus did. We do not know what happened to Lazarus. Tradition suggests that he was martyred; he would in any case die again. But his story lives on.

Mary took a pound of expensive perfume of pure nard, anointed Jesus's feet, and with her hair wiped his feet. (John 12:3a)

John had me with "expensive perfume," and "perfume" does sound better than the alternative translation "ointment." Ointment reminds me of what one puts on diaper rash or a sore muscle or a bug bite. The term for perfume or ointment comes from the same word as "myrrh" (as in the gifts of the magi, gold, frankincense, and myrrh). The term translated "pure" comes from the same Greek word-family as the term *pistis*, which means "faith" or "trust." Not only is the cost of the perfume over the top, so is Mary's wiping Jesus's feet with her hair. The image appears also in Luke 7:38, where for Luke, the woman, who was a sinner, is showing her gratitude for the forgiveness she finds in Jesus's presence. Mary's motive also appears to be gratitude, not for the forgiveness of sin, but for Jesus having restored her brother to life.

My students frequently approach this story with the view that Jesus is being "transgressive" or even "radically transgressive" in allowing Mary to touch him, since that would have been forbidden both by Jewish law and by Jewish custom. Wrong, and wrong. Anointing by a friend or relative is not a transgression but an effusive greeting. No one at the table with Jesus finds this act in John 12 weird; no one in antiquity would. John has already told us in 11:5 that Jesus "loved Martha and her sister and Lazarus," and Mary loves him in return. Everyone knew it. Nor is being anointed by a woman for one's burial a transgressive act. To the contrary, both men and women prepared corpses for burial in both Jewish and Gentile society. This business about the transgressive Jesus is just another example of trying to make Jesus look good by making Jewish culture look bad.

Other students see the point about the hair, which John may have borrowed from Luke 7, to be sensual—their next move is to reject that association, for heaven forbid Jesus would appreciate a sensual touch. While I understand this reaction, I think that John would appreciate the sensual reading. Jesus is an incarnate human being: he knows what it is like to be thirsty and tired (John 4:6). The transcendent meaning of language does not erase mundane connotations. He would appreciate a healing touch from a good friend.

Nor, by the way, need loose hair signal eroticism. Loose hair in antiquity was also associated with mourning, for when one mourns, there is no reason to engage in any form of beautification, such as pinning up one's hair or braiding it. As with the Samaritan woman at the well, who for generations was understood to be a "fallen woman," we see what we want to see, and far too often we see problems where there are none to be seen.

As long as we are speaking about body parts, we might also note the attention to feet. My mother's father owned a shoe store, which after my grandfather died my father managed. For a while, both of my children sold shoes at an upscale department store in Nashville. I know from shoes. John 12 reminds me of John the Baptizer's comment that he is unworthy to untie the strap from Jesus's sandal (John 1:27). Mary did not, as far as I can tell, think about "worthy" or "being unworthy," which to me puts her a step (the metaphor is deliberate) ahead of John. Providing a service or manifesting love should not be a matter of worth. I didn't like John's statement of lack of worth; I also don't like the comparable statement made by the centurion in Matthew 8:8 that "I am not worthy that you [Jesus] would come under my roof." I prefer we all begin with a sense of worth. Relative worth is fine; a sense of complete lack of worth strikes me as unhealthy.

Rather than internalize a lack of worth, an internalization that may have kept John from ministering to Jesus, we might take a page from Mary's playbook and begin with a sense of worth, of competence, and of agency. We can provide service to others. Moreover, people are so worthy that, in the next chapter, Jesus will wash their feet. Yes, we are human; yes, our feet are not necessarily the cleanest, or sweetest smelling, part of our body. But they are our feet, just as much in the divine image as the rest of us. They can remind us of Isaiah 52:7, the recognition of the beauty of the "feet of the one bringing good news" (Septuagint: the Greek word translated "bringing good news" is from the same root as *euangelion*, the word we translate "gospel") of peace and salvation. Every part of us is deserving of love. I would prefer, despite its Eucharistic usage in some churches, to leave the language of "We're not worthy" to reruns of "Wayne's World."

Mary also raises the question of how we show gratitude. The corporeality of the verse—feet, anointing, wiping with hair—is visceral. While speaking of Jesus as "the Word" can sound abstract, John's focus is also on Incarnation, the taking on of flesh. Jesus is about to die the most painful death; here he can enjoy the most luxurious of ministrations. The corporeality of the scene coupled with its connecting of life and death, anointing and crucifixion, is reinforced by the second part of John 12:3, where the smell of death is contrasted with the aroma of life.

When we continue to read in John's Gospel and come in the next chapter to Jesus washing the feet of the disciples, Mary's action should be recollected. The action is the same, but the import changes. Mary modeled gratitude; Jesus will model not just service but enslavement. Mary will remain grateful—this is her last scene in the Gospel—but following the washing of the disciples' feet, Jesus will take up his role as master and lord.

Jesus's action of service to others will be recollected whenever people can serve others, and others can with gratitude, and with no expectations of reciprocity, receive that service.

The house was filled with the fragrance of the perfume. (John 12:3b)

Our sense of smell is less acute, by as much as one hundred thousand times, as that of our dogs (that's fine; what my dog likes to smell is often not something that draws me close). But nor should our sense of smell be ignored. Our olfactory sense is substantially part of our nervous system—it operates on us apart from the intellect; it works on us even when we do not want it to do so.

The scent of the perfume directly contrasts with Martha's concern that, at the tomb, "already there is a stink, because it is the fourth day [since he has been in the tomb]" (John 11:39). The good scents bring good thoughts. On the rare occasions I get a whiff of the perfume my mother wore (Arpège), memories come flooding back. The smell of a secondhand or antique bookstore, or of fresh garlic simmering in olive oil…numerous memories, mostly very good. The scent of the perfume can also remind us of the scent of the Temple, where incense offerings were made. Speaking of the wilderness tabernacle, Exodus 40:27 describes Moses as having "offered fragrant incense."

According to Genesis 8:21, when God smelled the scent of the sacrificial offering Noah prepared (i.e., good barbecue), God promised never again to curse the ground. From smell comes reprieve. The first human olfactory image in the Bible concerns Isaac, who is tricked by his wife, Rebekah, and their younger twin, Jacob: Jacob pretends to be his brother, Esau, a man more comfortable in the fields than at home, by dressing in his clothes. Isaac is blind, so he relies at first on his olfactory senses. Jacob "approached and kissed [Isaac], and [Isaac] smelled the smell of his garments and blessed him, and said, 'See [an odd word choice!], the smell of my son is like the smell of a field that the Lord has blessed'" (Genesis 27:27). Without our other senses, the use of one only can be misleading.

There are other smells, such as the stink Martha warns Jesus about at the tomb, the mere thought of which can make us feel nauseous. In describing the first plague, when the waters turn to blood, Exodus 7:18 remarks, "The fish that are in the river will die, the river will stink, and the Egyptians will not be able to drink water from the river." Today's ecological concerns find ancient analogies. Isaiah 3:24 is one of several verses concerning the devastation of war, when "instead of spice there will be a decay."

We can read John through seeing and hearing and tasting; we can also smell our way through the Gospel—the wine at Cana (oenophiles call the smell of wine the "nose"), the loaves and fishes in the wilderness, the mud mixed with spittle.... Everything becomes more alive. But we cannot rely on one sense alone, or like Isaac, we may be misled.

But Judas Iscariot, one of his disciples, the one about to hand him over, says, "Why was this perfume not sold for three hundred denarii and given to the poor?" (John 12:4-5)

In the Synoptic accounts, Judas is not the one who complains about the expense of the perfume. In Mark the complainers are "some" at the table; in Matthew, the disciples; in Luke, the Pharisee, in internal monologue, complains about the woman's attending to Jesus. John specifies the woman is Mary and the complainant is Judas. He threatens to spoil the scene. Aromatherapy and a massage cannot compensate for a traitor, especially one who poses as a friend. In English, we sometimes use the word *stinker* to refer to someone who behaves in an offensive manner. The nineteenth century gives us the religiously inclined "stink to high heavens." We speak of "smelling a rat" when we sense someone is up to no good; when "something smells fishy" the issue is something false rather than Dover sole. The "smell test" is designed to distinguish false from true claims, or whether something is too good to be true.

Our senses can again deceive us. Judas has a point: Why waste money on perfume when one can give to charity? But his words are also deceptive, since in the next verse John tells us that Judas, a thief, was interested in keeping the money for himself (12:6). "Stinker" seems like the right adjective.

And yet, that point about the worth of the ointment finds its own textual resonances both in earlier stories and in later ones. The wedding at Cana, with its description of the best wine, holds a sense of expensive wine, like that expensive eschatological banquet with rich wine and meat and marrow. Nothing is too good when it comes to the celebration of divine love. More, the expense of the perfume (*myron*) is mirrored by the expense of the one hundred pounds of myrrh (*smyrna*) with which Joseph of Arimathea and Nicodemus bury Jesus (John 19:39), and no one complains about this royal burial. People choose how they want to spend their money—what is generous to one person is a waste to another. John makes us think about how and where we want to invest.

She kept it...for the day of my burial. (John 12:7)

The short scene for John concludes with Jesus's affirming Mary's action, as he affirms the woman in the related Synoptic scenes. The scent of Mary's anointing will be recollected at the tomb, when Nicodemus and Joseph of Arimathea entomb Jesus with one hundred pounds of myrrh and aloes (John 19:39). It should be recollected when people return to the churches of their youth, and the smell of the sanctuary, or the youth lounge, or the fellowship hall, brings back good memories. The Roman Catholic tradition speaks of the "odor of sanctity," often said to smell like roses, or flowers, that arises from the bodies of saintly people, especially at their deaths.

To embalm a body, or to bury it with myrrh and aloes, is meant to keep away the scent of death. Perhaps instead that smell should be welcomed, since death will come to us all, even Jesus. It cannot be perfumed over. Jesus affirms this fact.

A final thought: as I am writing this chapter, next to me is a scented candle that my daughter bought for me. I suspect whenever I encounter this scent again, I'll think of writing this chapter and so of Mary's anointing. Memories add to memories, and when we inhale, the spirit moves, and recollection comes unbidden.

The Foot Washing (John 13:1-20)

John pairs the story of Nicodemus, the leader of the Pharisees who comes to Jesus by night and never quite achieves that "born anew" status, with the Samaritan woman who encounters Jesus at noon and becomes the first successful evangelist. John also pairs the man by the pool of Bethsaida, who remains an outsider, with the man Jesus tells to wash in the pool of Siloam, who becomes a witness, and John pairs the story of Mary's anointing of Jesus's feet for his burial with the story of Jesus's washing the feet of the disciples to model for them the importance of mutual service. The scenes help interpret each other, and the comparison makes our understanding richer.

Before the Festival of the Passover (John 13:1a)

Again, John gives us a temporal indicator: the last supper Jesus will share with his disciples takes place before the Passover. For the

Fourth Gospel, the supper is not a seder, a Passover meal. Instead, John locates Jesus's crucifixion at the time the lambs for the Passover meal are being sacrificed in the Temple. For John, Jesus is the new Passover lamb. The mention of the Passover also returns us to Mary's anointing, set in 12:1 at another supper "six days before the Passover."

In between these two meals, Jesus entered Jerusalem and has been greeted by the people from the city who were carrying palm fronds (hence the designation "Palm Sunday") and hailing him as king. He has provided a model of prayer for his followers, but in a manner distinct from the Synoptic accounts. While the Synoptic depiction of Jesus has him pray that the cup of death be removed from him (Matthew 26:39; Mark 14:36; Luke 22:42), John 12:27 recognizes that while Jesus is troubled, he also asks, "What should I say: 'Father, save me from this hour?'" Then he answers his own question, "But it is on account of this that I have come to this hour."

While Matthew (27:46) and Mark (15:34) portray Jesus on the cross as reciting the first line of Psalm 22, "My God, my God, why have you forsaken me?" the Johannine Jesus, who states, "I and the Father are one" (10:30), would never suggest any feeling of abandonment. These distinctions do not make one text right and one wrong; to the contrary, they give us multiple pictures of Jesus. At times, disciples need someone who also knows what it is like to feel abandoned by God and yet perseveres by reciting a psalm; at times, they need someone who fully models the indwelling of the divine that allows all things to be possible. Theology, or Christology, is not something that can be constrained to a single model, for that would limit the power of the divine to be what it will be. The remainder of John 12 develops both the divine identity of Jesus and the inability of some people to believe in him.

Then, in chapter 13, he turns from public pronouncement to private teaching. The following chapters are for his followers, at that time and into the future.

Jesus knew that his hour had come to depart from this world and go to the Father. Having loved his own who were in the world, to the end he loved them. (John 13:1b)

The hour has come. The hour had already been in place since close to the beginning of the Gospel. Jesus had told the Samaritan woman that "the hour is coming and is now here" (John 4:23) when worshippers will worship the Father in spirit and truth. In 5:25, he tells the "Jews," that the "hour is coming and now is," when the dead will hear the voice of the Son of God, and those who hear will live. The verse anticipates the general resurrection of the dead, but it is also a condemnation of those who do not, or cannot because they are not called, hear that voice. For John's Gospel, the nondisciple is already dead; the disciple is already resurrected to new life.

The hour for John is not clock time, *chronos* time. It comes whenever anyone makes a decision to follow Jesus, or not. Every hour can be *that* hour. The Gospel gives a both/and meaning to salvation and damnation: followers do not need to wait until they die, or until a general resurrection of the dead. They are already alive. The converse regarding those who are not numbered among the followers also holds. Followers today will need to determine if they accept John's hour, or if they opt for a more pluralistic approach to salvation, as, for example, Paul offers in Romans 11:26, when he states that "all Israel"—by which he means "all Jews"—will be saved.

A related aspect of this hour, concerning a more pluralistic vision, appears in John 12:21, following Mary's anointing of Jesus's feet and the Jesus's entry into Jerusalem, when "Greeks" (that is, Gentiles), come to Philip, "who was from Bethsaida in Galilee" and request to see Jesus. John introduced Philip in 1:43-45, where, in typical Johannine fashion, one person conveys information to another. Jesus first encounters Philip and commands, "Follow me." After noting that Bethsaida was the city of Andrew and Peter, John then recounts how Philip told Nathanael that Jesus was the one of whom Moses and the prophets had spoken. Now Philip is the one to bring the Greeks to Jesus, an allusion to the Gentile mission promoted by the disciples. Philip tells Andrew and Peter, who convey the Greeks' interest to Jesus. Now Jesus announces, "The hour has come when the Son of Humanity will be glorified" (John 12:23). The glorification, which is also the crucifixion, comes when some Gentiles take their place as "his own."

In retrospect, John 13:1 may also provide an explanation of John 10:16, part of the good shepherd discourse, where Jesus announces, "I have other sheep that are not of this court (i.e., not of this fold). It is necessary that I bring them also, and they will listen to my voice. And there will be one flock, one shepherd." An allusion to the good shepherd discourse in chapter 13 is also supported by the reference to "his own" in John 13:1, which recalls John 10:3-4, "The doorkeeper opens [the door] for him, and the sheep hear his voice, and he calls his own sheep by name and leads them out. When he has brought out all his own, he goes ahead of them, and the sheep follow him because they know his voice."

The idea of the single shepherd, another image for the God of Israel, as the famous Psalm 23 recounts with "The Lord is my shepherd," is necessarily for a monotheistic (one God) tradition. The single flock might be nuanced, because I would not want to lose human distinctiveness—either now or in the future. Daniel 7:14 speaks about the "one like a son of humanity" (or an angel but in human form) whom "all peoples, nations, and languages should serve." Similarly, John the seer of Revelation 7:9 reports that he saw "a great crowd . . . from all nations and tribes and peoples and languages, standing before the throne and before the Lamb." Ethnic and cultural distinctiveness are not erased but are celebrated.

Regarding the love Jesus expresses in John 13:1, it appears distinct from the love God shows in the famous John 3:16, "God so loved the world." The Johannine Jesus does not personally express this universal love. Instead, he "loved *his own* who were in the world." I see here also a distinction between the Johannine Jesus, who loves his own, and the Jesus of the Synoptics, who demands that his disciples love not only insiders and not even only outsiders but also enemies: "Love your enemies and pray for those who persecute you" (Matthew 5:44 and see Luke 6:27, 35).

On the other hand, compared to the Synoptic Gospels, John emphasizes the love Jesus has for those who are his own, a group that includes the disciples but excludes Judas, who has shown himself to be a thief. Thus, Jesus's love will continue for his own, despite Peter's failure to support him and Thomas's doubting. The disciples are not required to be perfect, and failures of faith, even betrayal, can be recuperated. No matter what the faithful do, once they are part of the system, already chosen by God, they will not lose Jesus's love. In this way, Jesus reminds me of a loving parent: no matter what the child does, the parent continues to love the child. Such love does not ignore responsibility, but it prevails.

When John states that Jesus "loved them to the end," we have a paradox, since the end of this love never occurs. It is infinite, timeless. There is no reason to presume that the love would cease following a last judgment. The Greek term translated "end" is *telos*, as in the term "teleology." The same word occurs in Romans 10:4, where Paul proclaims the Christ to be the *telos* of the law. Paul's point is not that with the Christ the Torah is now dismissed; to the contrary, Paul's point is that the Christ is the goal of the law, that to which the law points. We can, with some linguistic generosity given Paul's language, gloss John's point with the idea that this love is the goal of discipleship, to infinity and beyond (okay, not logical, but rhetorically effective).

At the same time John expresses Jesus's unconditional love for those who are his own, we learn that Satan had already "put it in the heart of Judas son of Simon Iscariot to betray him" (John 13:2). Judas is in the presence of Jesus, who epitomizes love, and he can neither feel it himself nor receive it.

Jesus, knowing that the Father had given all things into his hands, and that he had gone out from God and was going to God..." (John 13:3)

Jesus can present himself in utter humiliation to his followers because he knows his true origin and nature. John 13:3 both reminds us of the Gospel's opening—that the Word was God—and also alludes to Philippians 2:6-11, which locates Jesus in the heavens and in the divine form and then depicts his *kenosis*, his self-emptying into the form of one enslaved and one who dies on a cross. At the end of this passage from Philippians, often called the "Christ hymn" (athough it sounds more like a creed than a song), Jesus is restored to divine glory. The point for both John and Philippians is not only christological but also anthropological. Those who know that they are children of God, those who know that the love of God will last until the end, can endure all. The role of being enslaved is temporary; being a child of God is permanent.

John and Paul insist that our origins have some bearing on our present. This attention to history strikes me as increasingly important. I've had students inform me that history is bunk (they are quoting Henry Ford; I doubt that they know they are quoting; I'm also not sure they know who Henry Ford was). For them, the only thing that matters is what they have experienced. A few students take the next step and insist that because history as we have it is written by the historical winners, we cannot trust reconstructions of the past. I find these comments at best unfortunate. In 1905, George Santayana stated, "Those who cannot remember the past are condemned to repeat it." To extend his point: those who do remember the past know what is worth saving, what must be regretted or atoned for, what might be recuperated.

These points help us with John 13:3: If we know our origins, we can also tap into the experiences and the strengths of those who came before us, whether that "us" is defined by the family, the gender, ethnicity, ability, and so on, since we all have multiple identities. We can also learn from how members of our group, however defined, found themselves both oppressors and the oppressed. And if we know we are children of God and have a sense that our future lies with God, then we are in a better position not only to endure but also to grow, to create, and to improve.

[Jesus] got up from supper, and took off his garment, and tied a cloth around himself. (John 13:4)

John 13:2 identifies the scene as a supper. Had we been thinking of the Synoptic Gospels, we may have been expecting the Last Supper, where Jesus takes bread and wine and then speaks of his body and blood, although John has already addressed such Eucharistic concerns in the bread of life discourse in chapter 6. Plus, 13:1 states that the festival of the Passover had not yet begun. This meal anticipates the Passover even as it sends us back to the initial wedding feast at Cana, the feeding of the five thousand, and the previous chapter where Jesus reclined at table and Mary anointed his feet. Any meal can recall or anticipate others; any table can be a site of revelation, or of service.

When Jesus removes himself from the supper, he is not play-acting but setting an example. John could have simply noted that Jesus washed the disciples' feet; instead, John details the actions. Jesus rises himself from the table where he had been host. He changes from participating in a meal to enacting a service. He strips off his outer garment, which means he would have been naked save for a cloth covering his genitals. He thus makes himself both exposed and vulnerable. He appears not a lord but as one enslaved. Finally, he ties a towel around his waist, which he can then use to wipe the feet of his disciples. John details the divestment, the change of garments, the careful preparation.

The scene is extraordinary, and when I read the Gospel, I often find it more remarkable than John's account of the Crucifixion. While the Johannine Jesus orchestrates his arrest and crucifixion, and he clearly has the ability to stop both, in these later cases his opponents play a role. For this scene in John 13, he is on his own. More, I think I would find it more difficult to show such vulnerability and servitude in front of people who looked up to me or depended on me—my students, my children—than before strangers.

And at the same time, this careful washing reminds me of the times when I could not care for myself and someone took care of me, in all my vulnerability. When I was in the hospital because of a nasty bout of endocarditis, my husband, my children, and my friends literally "took care" of me, both in spirit and in body. There is no way I can ever reciprocate their kindness, and, in the wonderful way the world works, they do not expect such reciprocation. We might also think of how we were cared for as infants, when we were wiped and washed and powdered, in acts which, if we were lucky in the parent department, came with unconditional love.

Finally, this will not be the only time Jesus will be without his garment. The Roman soldiers will strip his clothes from his body (19:23). From the cross, Jesus again will "serve" those who follow him, but the soldiers miss the point. The foot washing anticipates the cross in multiple ways. Each time we read John 13, we may find more.

Then he poured water into a washbasin and began to wash the disciples' feet and to wipe them with the cloth that was tied around him. (John 13:5)

Sometimes texts strike me by what they do not say. On the few occasions when I've had a professional pedicure, I've first taken my shoes off. Why no mention of the sandals in John 13? I'm also a textual nerd, so when I think of washing feet, I also think of John the Baptist—bear with me—who announces in John 1:27 that he is not worthy to untie the strap of Jesus's sandal. Here it will be Jesus who takes off the sandal of the first disciple to receive his ministrations. I suspect the others took off their sandals on their own. The reversal is complete: John expresses his lack of worth to take off a shoe; Jesus paradoxically shows his worth, and the worth of service, by removing the shoes of his disciples and then washing their feet. Following Philippians 2:7, he "humbles himself, taking the form of one enslaved."

Like the parable of the good Samaritan in Luke 10, where the action slows down to describe in detail the Samaritan's action of binding wounds, pouring oil and wine on them (it sounds to me like salad dressing, but the combination was regarded as medicinal), placing the wounded man on the donkey, and so on, so John details Jesus's actions. He has prepared himself with the cloth, he pours the water, he begins to wash, he wipes not with his hair but with the towel around his waist.

The timing means that as he attends to the first disciple, the other eleven must be wondering what Jesus is doing, and why. They have the chance to speak with one another, although John offers no details. Did they question? Demur? Complain? Were they completely flabbergasted?

Or perhaps, when John's Gospel was read aloud in a house church in Ephesus or Athens or Rome, did the enslaved members of the household think to themselves, "That is what we do. No one has ever noticed the details." Did they find their actions acknowledged and affirmed? Or did they resent the fact that Jesus will put his robe back on, return to the table, and take his seat as host, while they remain with a basin of dirty water and a cloth stained with the dust from the road? Did they wonder if anyone would wash their feet, and if they did, did they anticipate a one-off, or a complete change in relationships?

Today, various churches hold foot washing ceremonies on the Thursday of Holy Week. For example, in 2023, Pope Francis went to a youth penitentiary outside Rome where he not only washed the feet of ten men and two women (one of whom was a Muslim and several were immigrants to Rome), he also kissed their feet, here in imitation of the woman "who was a sinner," in Luke 7:38. This is a lovely blending of stories. The Pope both takes the role of Jesus in washing and wiping the feet of those who do not have a position of authority comparable to his, and the role of the woman who kisses the feet of Jesus. His action put the recipients into the roles of both the disciples (in John's Gospel) and Jesus (in Luke's Gospel). I would like to know what these youth thought following the event.

In some settings, members of a congregation wash one another's feet. That way, all both serve and receive service. When we recollect Mary's loving action, together with the service Jesus provides, we can get a better sense of the intimacy of the action—the touch of hands on feet, of water on flesh, of the cloth wiping away the water.

He came to Simon Peter. He says him, "Lord, are you going to wash my feet?" (John 13:6)

I want to know what Andrew, Philip, Nathanael, and the others were thinking at this point. Were they too afraid to say anything, as they were afraid to say anything when they saw Jesus having a conversation with a woman back in Sychar (John 4:27)? And what was Judas thinking, given that the decision to betray Jesus has already been made. Sometimes external washing has no effect on internal purity. Not all rituals have meaning.

Peter asks a very good question, just as the woman asked Jesus a good question about how he was going to get that running water without a bucket. Jesus has offered Peter a sign, and it is one that requires interpretation. Granted, John does not call this event a "sign"; it is not a change in the natural world, as is turning water into wine or raising the dead. But if we take seriously the idea of the Incarnation, then the scene can also be seen as miraculous: the scene is another example of God not only wanting to be in relationship with us and not only functioning in the role of parent but also functioning in the role of one enslaved. Deliberately to choose humility over pride, serving over being served, strikes me as contrary to our natural way of functioning in the world and thus, in a sense, miraculous.

Peter's address "lord" (*kyrie*) is spot on, since "lords" are not usually in the role of washing people's feet. That is the task for the enslaved, for a servant, and in some settings for children or for women in the household. To wash someone's feet is to take a subordinate role, and it would be weird, at best, for a hierarchically superior person voluntarily to self-subordinate. Peter is confused. Rightly so.

Jesus answered, "You do not know now what I am doing, but after these things you will know." (John 13:7)

I recall hearing at various stages of my life, "You'll understand later." "Why, I asked the head of the math department of my high school, do I need to learn trigonometry?" His response, "You'll understand." I never did. On the other hand, some things cannot be understood except in retrospect. Only when we get to the end of the story or the movie or our lives will we more fully be able to put things into perspective. What seems disjointed or arbitrary now becomes consistent and logical later on. Age and experience can bring with them greater clarity, or better nuance (and hence the concern again for knowing history, since the historical reconstruction will change based on new knowledge and new experience).

John does not return to this scene, so we readers must determine what Peter, at the end of the Gospel, will understand. The options are several. Later in the chapter, Jesus will put his garment back on, recline at table to eat, and explain, "If therefore I, the Lord and the teacher, have washed your feet, you ought to wash one another's feet, for I have given you an example so that just as what I did for you, even you should do" (John 13:14-15). The model here is one of mutuality and service. If Jesus, who is every way to Sunday superior to the disciples, can wash their feet, they can do the same with one another. The action can help the group find unity without competition.

Next, this is not the only model or pattern Jesus establishes for his disciples. When he dies for them, that death also become a model. If we give up our sense of superiority, not merely in our self-impression but also by our actions, we are in a better position to serve others and to put others before ourselves. The service enacted becomes muscle memory; it is something we do, ideally on a regular basis, rather than merely think about.

The connection of John 13 to Jesus's death is not only anticipated by Mary's having anointed his feet, which Jesus reads as an anointing for burial (John 12:7), it is secured toward the end of the chapter, when in 13:34, Jesus speaks of giving the disciples a "new commandment" which is "That you love one another. Just as I have loved you, so that you should love one another." The command to "love one another" is not what is new; it is as old as its first iteration, in Leviticus 19:18, "You shall love your neighbor as yourself," and Leviticus 19:34, "You shall love the *ger* (the Hebrew suggests the not-native-born, or in today's context, the sojourner, migrant, immigrant) who lives among you, because you were *gerim* (the plural of *ger*) in the land of Egypt." According to Rabbi Akiva, executed by the Romans about a century after Jesus, love of neighbor is the principal commandment in Torah.

What is new here, a point that John will explain two chapters later, is what "just as I have loved you" implies. Peter cannot realize the point yet, but he will. In John 15:12-13, Jesus elaborates on his "commandment, that you should love one another just as I have loved you. No one has greater love than this, to give one's life on behalf of one's friends." We may tell people that we love them, but whether we are willing to die for them raises the stakes. Parents may well volunteer to die in the place of their children, or spouses for each other. Once outside the family, the price becomes more exorbitant. But the love behind the willingness to die for another is unmistakable.

There are other matters to ponder from the foot washing. For example, Jesus had taken on the role of a subordinate, whether servant or enslaved. One takeaway is that he models for his disciples what has been called "servant leadership." The point is not only that one is to serve others, it is to do so without expectation of return, even without gratitude, since in Greco-Roman households, the enslaved were generally not "thanked" for doing what was expected of them. For the disciples, the reward is in the service and is the service. Second, the washing has import for the person who receives the service. Those who have their feet washed by disciples are to feel worthy, to feel themselves recognized as children of God. They are *seen*.

Because the action recapitulates Mary's anointing, the foot washing can also be seen as honoring the child of God in all of us. Jesus does for Peter in effect what Mary did for him. The service is one of generosity, whether with water or oil, whether from the tap or from the spa. More, the foot washing honors the human body, not just the head or the hands, but the dusty, dirty, calloused feet that also need, and too often rarely receive, attention. And Peter will learn even more, although it will take some time.

Peter says to him, "No, never ever will you wash my feet." Jesus answered him, "Unless I wash you, you have no share with me." Simon Peter says to him, "Lord, not my feet only but also the hands and the head." (John 13:8-9)

I know John 13 is a solemn lesson about service, a very difficult view of the Incarnate deity in a servile position, and an anticipation of the cross. And then Peter's comment. I think had I been in a house church, perhaps toward the end of a meal, and someone were telling John's story, when the enactor got to "also the hands and the head," I would have burst out laughing. Peter so misses the mark. John has had moments of humor throughout, and this is another example. Artistically, the line relieves the tension and the sense of tragedy; pedagogically, laughter allows us better to receive the difficult lessons: Jesus is going to die, his body has already been anointed, he is about to be betrayed, and the same fate may befall those who claim to be his disciples.

Jesus explains that the head and hands are not necessary: the washing is symbolic of humility and a model of service. Then the subject turns to Judas, who has been at the supper the whole time; Jesus will have washed his feet alongside the feet of the other disciples. But Judas is possessed by Satan. External ritual is designed to have internal transformation. Otherwise, running water is just running water and a draft is just wind.

While Judas has no interest in understanding what Jesus is doing, Peter wants to understand but at present cannot. Nor does he yet understand the connection of service to cross. At the end of the chapter, he assures Jesus that he will "give [his] life [*psychē*, which could also mean 'soul']" for him (John 13:37). Jesus instead predicts that Peter will deny him three times before the rooster crows (13:38).

And yet, at the end of the Gospel, there is reconciliation and understanding. Peter's threefold denial is matched by his threefold insistence that he loves his Lord (John 21:15-17). Jesus then offers a veiled prediction of Peter's own death, "When you grow old (*gēraskō*, the same root as "geriatric"), you will stretch out your hands, and another will dress you and bring you where you do not want to go" (John 21:18b).

Following the foot washing, Jesus tells Peter, "Where I am going, you are not able to follow me now, but you will follow afterward (John 13:36). In the epilogue, Jesus tells Peter, after predicting Peter's death, "Follow me" (John 21:22). Only at the end of the story, after the report of Jesus's resurrection, does the meaning of this following become clear: Peter will follow with a life of evangelization and signs, of service and of martyrdom. He is both called and willing to accept the invitation; he is both fearful and assured; he is both a flawed human being and a beloved child of God. I suspect that each time he took off his sandals, he thought of that foot washing. And he was renewed.

While the New Testament does not report Peter's death, early Christian stories depict him as traveling to Rome, where he is executed. Unwilling, and thinking himself unworthy, to die the same death as his Lord, he asks to be crucified upside down.

CHAPTER 6

Mary Magdalene and Doubting Thomas

(John 20)

John 20 features, along with Jesus and appearances by the disciples, Mary Magdalene and Thomas. Each scene contains a doubt, a revelation, and a model for other followers. Each speaks how Jesus was was in his own time and is in our own time misunderstood, and each offers a corrective that concerns both Christology and ethics. Each is also in its own way a type of comedy, not in the sense of "ha ha" or even the smiles that could occur when the man in chapter 9 asks Jesus's opponents if they too want to be disciples, or when Peter insists on what looks like a sponge bath in John 12. The stories are comedies in the Aristotelian sense. While we do not have his treatise on comedy from the *Poetics*, we can reconstruct the parts: attention to human weakness, the resolution of rivalries and tensions, the corrections of mistakes, the restoration of community.

On (day) one of the Sabbaths, Mary the Magdalene came, in the morning, it still being dark, to the tomb. (John 20:1a)

Jesus's hour has come, and it remains. It was, and it now is, and it will always be. While clock time, *chronos* time, continues, the *kairos* time of Jesus also marks the hours. All time has become sacralized. The first day of the week is Sunday, since the Jewish week ends Saturday evening, when three stars appear in the sky. But the first day is also the first day of a new time, a *kairos* time, marked by Jesus's resurrection. The time is now, but Mary does not know this yet.

The time is literally not "the first day" but "day one." That counting notice fits nicely here: time has had a reset; we are again at "day one," as we were "in the beginning" of John 1:1, and of Genesis when God said, "Be light."

To count days according to the Sabbath has the implications of sacralizing the entire week. We can begin Sunday, day one or the first day of the week, with the renewal that the Sabbath rest the day before, the seventh day, provides. We start day one rested and refreshed. And, we can anticipate the next Sabbath, and the next. To focus on the Sabbath means that all days take a sense of meaning from that Sabbath day. The count also sends us back to Genesis, to the distinct aspects of creation and that original day of rest. I find Genesis 1:1–2:4, with its sixth days of creation and a seventh of rest, a more optimistic way of counting than the nursery rhyme where "Wednesday's child is full of woe" and "Tuesday's child has far to go." I was born on a Friday, which is supposed to make me "loving and giving"; I can live with that. Better we check in with Genesis to see what happened on the day when we were born.

In the Fourth Gospel, we met Mary Magdalene in 19:25, where John locates her at the foot of the cross, together with Jesus's mother, his mother's sister (who may or may not be Mary the wife of Clopas— whether John gives us three women or four remains a crux in Gospel studies), and the Beloved Disciple. Mary stayed the course; unlike Peter, she did not deny Jesus, and she did not flee. The designation "Magdalene" has traditionally been understood as a reference to the city of Magdala (perhaps the place known by the Greek designation Tarichaea), located on the Sea of Galilee.

The name comes from the Hebrew for (big) "tower," so "Mary the Tower" is a possible reading. Yet for John in particular, I like the geographical reference. Mary takes her place alongside "Philip...from Bethsaida, the city of Andrew and Peter" (1:44), the people at the

Cana wedding in John 2:1-11, the followers of Jesus assembled in Capernaum (2:12), the Samaritans in Sychar, the family in Bethany (John 11–12), the people at the Pools of Beth-something (John 5) and Siloam (John 9), Nathanael of Cana in Galilee (21:2), as well as the events in Jerusalem. Each time Jesus sets foot in a location, it becomes something new; the same point holds for every resident, every visitor.

More, naming someone by place of origin has, at least for me, a different connotation than naming someone on the basis of family, whether "wife of" or "father of...." Today, in the United States, when we introduce ourselves, many of us begin not with our parents' names or what they did, but where we were born. What does that location say about us, what stereotypes does it evoke, what potential did it grant us? Finally, today I cannot think of Magdala without thinking about Mary, although there are other fascinating remains of the site, including a first-century synagogue with a table for reading the Torah.

John's notice that it was still dark brings us back to Nicodemus at midnight and the Samaritan woman at noon: Mary splits the difference as she moves from darkness to light. It will, pardon the pun, dawn on her that Jesus has risen, but the recognition takes time, as it did with the Samaritan woman. It is still dark, but it will not remain so. It cannot remain so. This will be the first day of the week for Mary, and it is the first day of her new understanding of Jesus.

We might think of every day as day one, and on that day we gain new perspective on what happened day minus-one, or year minus-sixty. The present can always give new insight onto the past. It can anticipate the future, but it can never fully predict it.

On the other hand, the notice that Mary went to the tomb while it was still dark makes me nervous. I get nervous when I walk the dog at night. She might trip over an unseen branch; there may be thieves lurking in the bushes. More, Mary is going to a tomb—cue every Halloween movie where teenagers go to a graveyard at night and when things typically do not go well for those teenagers. In the other Gospels, several women (the names are not consistent) go to the tomb, so at least they have one another for comfort and protection. Mary seems to be alone.

And yet, in the next verse she runs to announce to Peter and the anonymous Beloved Disciple, "They have taken the Lord out of the tomb, and we do not know where they have put him" (20:2). "We"? "We who?" Perhaps John has recalled the Synoptic versions of the story and added in a hint of these other women. I'd like to think that Mary was not alone. So often we focus on the main character that we ignore others who may have been present: equally mourning the death of Jesus; equally seeking to be with him at the tomb. That little word *we*—which in Greek is a first-person plural suffix attached to a verb and so not as prominent as the English "we"—gives a hint of a deeper and richer story, of tales not told but able to be imagined.

And she saw the stone taken up from the tomb. (John 20:1b)

In John 11:39, Jesus commands Martha, "Take up the stone" from Lazarus's tomb. Here Martha demurs out of concern for the stink that would spew from a decomposing corpse. Mary Magdalene does not have the same problem, for the stone has already been removed. We do not know who rolled the stone away, perhaps an angel or an earthquake or Jesus himself. I'm not sure why it matters, but perhaps you have some thoughts on this. A rolled-away stone testifies to multiple possibilities: wrong tomb, grave robbers, Roman soldiers took the body; "the Jews" took the body, other potential followers took the body, angelic intervention, an initially bad seal. All signs require interpretation, just as all words take on distinct connotations when used in particular contexts.

Mary draws the logical conclusion: someone has stolen the body (Matthew 28:13-15 suggests that some developed this rumor): as we've noted, she runs to Peter and the "other disciple whom Jesus loved" and announces, "They have taken the Lord out of the tomb, and we do not know where they have put him." I disagree with those commentators who see this comment as a sign of Mary's weakness for having failed to recall the predictions of the Resurrection. Mary's announcement to the disciples is, first, another iteration of John's "come and see" motif, where one person brings another to Jesus. It is also eminently practical: there is strength in numbers, especially if one is dealing with either grave robbers or Roman soldiers. More, Peter and the other disciple do not disregard Mary's testimony; to the contrary, they race to the tomb. We can sense a repeat of the Samaritan woman, who questions what she has seen, and the townspeople heed her words.

The "they" who supposedly took the body goes unspecified: Soldiers? Grave robbers? People who sought the nails that impaled victims to the cross, nails that were supposed to have magical properties? Tomb attendants? The one conclusion Mary does not draw is that Jesus has been resurrected. While the Synoptic accounts have Jesus repeat the point that he will be raised (e.g., Mark 8:31, "and after three days rise again"), for John, the people who encounter Jesus will only understand the predictions after the Resurrection itself. For example, when Jesus states in John 2:19, "Destroy this temple, and in three days I will raise it," his interlocutors have no clue that he was talking about his own body. Thus, John 2:22 notes that "after he was raised from the dead, his disciples remembered that he has said this." Retrospection brings clarity; what we cannot understand today, we may understand tomorrow and better understand on the third day.

We readers who know the full story are in the same position as we were with the people at the wedding, with Nicodemus and the Samaritan woman, and with the other people Jesus encounters in the Gospel. We know more than the characters in the story. At the same time, we may want to identify with them and as they come to deeper understanding, our understanding might increase as well.

John does not tell us how Mary knew where to find Peter and the other disciple, but there may be a hint in John 19:27, the previous chapter. As he is dying, Jesus tells the disciple whom he loved, "Look, your mother," and John recounts "from that hour the disciple took her into his own" ['home' is missing in Greek but implied]. Given this disciple's knowledge of Jerusalem and ability to navigate the court of the high priest, he likely had a house in the city. There, again likely, the other followers of Jesus, men and women, would have gathered. Acts 12:12 locates the followers at the home of the mother of John Mark, perhaps the same location, perhaps not. Any place can be a house church or a refuge for disciples or a place of comfort.

Peter and the Beloved Disciple

Mary makes her announcement to Peter and the Beloved Disciple—I suspect, based on the continuation of John 20, that the other disciples were in the room, or at least the building. Perhaps she singled these two out. Perhaps if she did, she realized not only that the anonymous disciple had a special relationship to Jesus but also she may have known Peter's denial of Jesus. And she knew that Peter had returned to the other disciples; rehabilitation has already started. Jesus had stated that he keeps his own, and Mary paid attention.

Peter and the other disciple race to the tomb, with the other disciple arriving first. The Gospel has suggested a rivalry between the two. Were I Peter, or any of the other disciples for that matter, I might feel a tad miffed that I was not the one identified as "whom Jesus loved." On the other hand, Jesus has made clear his love for all his followers on numerous occasions. Jealousy is an unattractive response.

John 20:7 notes that the cloth that had wrapped Jesus's head was not found with the linen wrappings but was rolled up separately. Countless sermons conclude that the description concerns banquet etiquette: a rolled-up napkin indicates that one will return to dinner; a napkin on the floor indicates that the meal is done. Enhancing this view is the King James Version of John 20:7, which translates the Greek word *soudarion* not as cloth but as "napkin." Thus, commentators conclude that Jesus took the time to roll up his napkin to show that he would be back. While the reading can bring new meaning to any napkin, that is not what John's early readers gleaned from the details.

The word *soudarion* indicates a small cloth that was used for preparing corpses (see also John 11:44, describing Lazarus) and could function also as a handkerchief. In Luke 19:20, part of the parable of the pounds, it refers to a cloth in which the third enslaved man hid the master's money. In Acts 19:12, it refers to pieces of cloth with which people touched Paul and then used to heal and to exorcise demons. The "napkin" symbolism shows how stories take on lives of their own, especially when they are translated into different languages. Given John's love of wordplay, he would probably approve.

I admit to liking procedural dramas, whether *CSI* or *NCIS* or *SVU* or whatever. The clothes are a small clue that something more than grave-robbing is going on. Robbers of whatever smash and grab; they do not generally tidy up afterwards. That rolled cloth indicates that the tomb was not opened by robbers—but we do not yet know by whom, or why. Clues pile up upon clues, and only gradually do we see the full picture.

The Beloved Disciple looks into the tomb and sees the linen wrappings that had bound Jesus's corpse. He does not enter, but Peter does, only to see the same grave clothes. The reversal is a nice move to show the two as working together: Peter arrives to the tomb second, but he enters it first. Finally, the other disciple goes into the tomb and John 20:8 says, "He saw and believed." John does not, however, say *what* they believed. That the tomb was empty? That Jesus has been raised?

The disciple whom Jesus loved, like Peter and like Mary Magdalene, "did not as yet understand the Scripture, that he must rise from the dead" (John 20:9). John makes a similar point about the connection of belief in the Resurrection to understanding the Scripture back in 2:21, the verse concerning tearing down and building back the Temple. No verse in the Scriptures of Israel clearly points to a dying and rising Messiah; no verse clearly points to the death of a Messiah or to a second coming. However, the followers of Jesus, reading these ancient texts through their belief in the Resurrection, found what others had not, and could not, see. If one believes in Jesus as Lord, the entire Scriptures of Israel, from Genesis to the end, points to Jesus. If one does not so believe, the Scriptures do not so testify. Words, again, take on new meaning in light of new beliefs.

The last line of our vignette of the two men, before we return to Mary Magdalene, who has also at some point returned to the tomb, is that "the disciples went again to theirs"—yes, the Greek is that vague. Most translations have them returning to their "homes," but that's a problem since at least Peter lives in Capernaum in Galilee. I don't think he had a second home in Jerusalem or Bethany. The idea that at least one of them concluded that Jesus had been raised but then just went home seems very odd to me. I'd prefer to see him returning to the other disciples to convey this good news to them.

On the other hand, we could see this line as a prod to anyone who goes to church on Easter Sunday, sings the hymns and listens to the sermon and sees the joy...and then just goes home. There is no change of perspective, call to share the good news, recognition of the conquering of death. What changes, once one concludes that the tomb is empty?

And Mary stood outside the tomb, weeping. (John 20:11a)

Mary informs the two disciples that the tomb is empty, and the two men race to the tomb. Mary also returned to the tomb, although how and when she got there remains unnoted. I'd like to think that she ran alongside, or even outpaced Peter. Then as the two male disciples return, they leave Mary at the tomb. Did they speak with her, or she with them? Did they try to comfort her or convince her to return with them? Have we ever left mourners at a tomb, mourners who refuse to follow back to the parking lot the rest of the people attending the funeral? Did Mary ask them to stay with her, as "the Jews" stayed with Mary and Martha? John offers no dialogue here.

This is not the first time in the Gospel we have seen a woman named Mary weep at a tomb. In John 11:33, at the tomb of Lazarus, Jesus sees Mary, the sister of Martha and Lazarus, weeping, and with her the "Jews" who had come to comfort her. John 20 continues to be a variation on the theme of death and resurrection first sounded in John 11.

At Lazarus's tomb, Jesus asks, "Where have you put him?" (John 11:34a). The response is the familiar theme, "Lord, come and see" (11:34b). At this moment, John records the famous line "Jesus wept" (11:35). Whether he weeps in recognition of the pain the sisters and those who accompany them feel in the face of Lazarus's death, in recognition of the fact of death itself and so the fate of all people, to demonstrate his love for Lazarus (this is the conclusion the Jews draw upon seeing him weep), or for any other reasons, John does not detail. We each encounter death, and mourning, in our own way.

In John 20:13, when the angels in the tomb ask Mary Magdalene, "Woman, why are you weeping?" she explains that others have taken the body of Jesus, "and I do not know where they have put him." To Jesus, whom she suspects is the gardener, she similarly responds, "Lord/sir (*kyrie*), if you have carried him away, tell me where you have put him, and I will take him away" (John 20:15). In both stories the question is not simply "Where have you put him?" but more viscerally, "Where is he?" This is a question anyone can ask at a gravesite: where is the person I so loved? For John, the answer concerning any who follow Jesus is ultimately, "Not here in the ground," but somehow already risen, with Jesus.

As she was weeping, she leaned into the tomb. (20:11b)

Although John does not say that Mary entered the tomb, she nevertheless sees more than did Peter and the Beloved Disciple. Mary sees two angels in white, sitting where the body of Jesus had been put, one where his head had been, the other where his feet had been (20:12). She is at a distance, comparably speaking, from Peter and the other disciple, but she sees more.

The scene conveys both presence and absence. Seeing two angels is not something that happens on alternate Thursdays. Nor is it clear that Mary recognizes the two as angels. White garments are, for people at the time, suggestive of angels or even divinity (Daniel 7:9; 2 Maccabees 11:8; Matthew 28:3; and the Synoptic "Transfiguration" scenes [Matthew 17:2; Mark 9:3; and Luke 9:29]) but they can also indicate wealth (see Ecclesiastes 9:8). For Revelation 3:4-5, they signal worth and sanctity. Again, Mary must interpret.

The reference to the placement of the angels where Jesus's head and feet had been reminds me of two separate texts. The first is Engelbert Humperdinck's "Evening Prayer" from his opera "Hänsel and Gretel" (this is a different Engelbert Humperdinck [1854–1921] than the one who sang "Please release me"), with the line about being guarded by angels as we sleep. The notion that benevolent heavenly beings are with us, to guard and guide, can be comforting.

The other, and the more biblically relevant texts, are the scenes of the anointing of Jesus: two on his head (Matthew and Mark); two on his feet (Luke and John). The head and feet can also function as a *merismus*, the idea that the ends encompass everything in between. For example, "When in the beginning God created the heavens and the earth" (Genesis 1:1, the verse evoked in John 1:1, but here translating the Hebrew temporal clause), the heavens and the earth include everything in between. Thus, the angels stand for the entire body of Jesus; they mark its place. They even remind us of that heaven and earth connection in John 1:51, the only other reference to angels in the Gospel, where Jesus tells Nathanael, "You will see heaven opened and the angels of God ascending and descending on the Son of Humanity."

The body of Jesus (John 20:12 uses the Greek term *sōma*, which means "body" rather than the word that translates "corpse") is missing, but the angels are placeholders. The body does not need to be present for its *presence* to be felt. It can be experienced in paintings, in Eucharist, in the face of others. John is continuing to prepare disciples for when Jesus is not present in his own incarnate body.

The angels ask Mary why she is weeping. The answer should have been obvious, but perhaps to the angels it is not. They know why the body is missing; Mary does not. They are thinking in heavenly terms. Mary, like the Samaritan woman, needs to catch up. And she will.

The angels also address Mary as "woman" (*gynē*), and by that address recall Jesus's address to his mother in Cana, to the Samaritan at the well, to Mary the sister of Martha, and again to his mother at the cross. The address can function as an invitation to read Mary Magdalene at the tomb in light of these other accounts. From Cana comes the transformation of water into wine, as at the tomb the transformation of death to new life. From the well comes the woman, who brings the people of Sychar to belief in Jesus, just as Mary in John 20 will become the apostle to the apostles by proclaiming the Resurrection to the disciples hiding in fear.

The connections between the sisters in John 11 and Mary in John 20, which we've already detailed, show how John takes death very seriously, and so takes mourning seriously as well. Hope, indeed surety, of resurrection does not make the loss easier. Finally, the connection to the mother of Jesus at the cross shows that Mary Magdalene is not alone. She too is part of a larger group of people committed to one another in their commitment to Jesus.

Woman, why are you weeping? Whom do you seek? (John 20:15a)

After explaining to the angels that she wanted to know where Jesus's body was, Mary turns and sees Jesus. He asks her the same questions as did the angels. Heavenly minds think alike. He also adds, "Whom do you seek?" or "Whom are you looking for?" For John, the immediate response should be rather, "come and see." Mary will shortly get to this point.

Second, John explains that Mary does not recognize Jesus (20:14); rather, she supposed him to be the gardener. Multiple allusions are at play in this verse. First, it's not quite dawn, and moreover, she has been weeping. It's hard to see in the dark and through tears. But beyond the obvious, Mary does not recognize Jesus because, as far as she is aware, the last time she saw him he had died on the cross. Her mind cannot comprehend that she is seeing him in the flesh, as it were. The expression "I can't believe my eyes" comes to mind.

Third, the scene reminds us of the account in Luke 24 of the two on the road to Emmaus. These disciples cannot recognize Jesus, even though he is giving them an advanced Bible study as he walks beside them. Only in the breaking of bread—a Eucharistic allusion—do they realize whom they have seen, and now he is gone. Sight merges with touch and taste and hearing, and the vision cannot be sustained, save in the mind's eye.

Fourth, John is once again developing a literary convention, only to explode it. As the Samaritan woman at the well evokes biblical scenes of betrothals, so John 20 evokes a motif from the Hellenistic romance genre, where young lovers are separated, one thinks the other one is dead, there's a case of mistaken identity, and finally the lovers are reunited. Even Mary's concern to claim the body of Jesus fits into the genre. But then instead of getting married and living together happily ever after, Jesus and Mary separate, as he will ascend to his Father and she will go to the other disciples to proclaim what she has seen and heard. From John's Gospel, any conventional setting, whether a television procedural or a sitcom or a news broadcast, can be seen to have multiple layers and can open the possibility of bursting out of its walls.

Finally, Mary thinks Jesus is the gardener. This would be a normal response—she is in a garden. We should be no more surprised that Mary talks with this supposed gardener than we should be surprised that the mother of Jesus speaks with the catering director or Mary and Martha speak to Jesus at the tomb. Men and women speaking with each other would be perfectly normal, unless, as we saw in our discussion of John 4, one happens to be a Jew and the other a Samaritan.

But this is not a normal setting. The reference to the gardener sends me back to Genesis 2, where the first human being, "the-adam" (Hebrew *ha-adam*) is placed in a garden, to till it and to guard it. In this new garden, with a different man and woman, we are back in Eden, and again we have a reset where, in this *kairos*-time, disobedience is not the next step; love is.

The reference to gardens and gardeners also sends me back to John 12:23, where Jesus announces, "The hour has come for the Son of Humanity to be glorified," and then to the next verse, an agricultural image of how a grain of wheat falls to the earth and dies, and because it dies, it is able to bear much fruit. Jesus is both gardener and seed, dead and now alive.

Jesus says to her, "Mariam." (John 20:16)

The direct address returns us to John 10:3, the good shepherd discourse, where Jesus states, "The sheep hear his voice, and he calls his own sheep by name and he leads them out." Jesus thus acknowledges Mary as one of his own, which despite her presence at the cross is not an identification the Gospel had previously made. There are additional connections between this first resurrection scene and in John 20 to this earlier speech. For example, John 10:4 states that the sheep follow Jesus "because they know his voice" and in 10:27, Jesus states, "my sheep hear my voice. I know them, and they follow me." It is by his voice—by his *word*—that Mary now encounters the risen Jesus. John 10:14 anticipates this recognition when Jesus announces, "I am the good shepherd, and I know my own and my own know me." In the next verse, 10:15, Jesus speaks about laying down his life for the sheep, as he had done for his followers in John 19.

The call by name also reminds me of John 11:43, where Jesus cries with a loud voice, "Lazarus, come out!" Whereas here in John 20, it is Jesus who has come out of the tomb; it is Mary who needs to move from the image of Jesus dying on the cross to the image of Jesus in full vitality standing before her. Finally, I think back to John 1:42, where Jesus says to Peter: "You are Simon son of John. You will be called Cephas [from *kepha*, Aramaic for 'rock']" and John adds that the name "is translated Peter" (that is, "rock" in Greek, as in "petrified" or "turned to stone"). We are called by name, and sometimes we are renamed. So too with Jesus, whether called "Rabbi" or "Rabbouni" or "Lord" or "Word." No name fully encompasses any of us.

I would have expected Jesus to call Mary "woman." Instead, the personal name appears. She is now to come fully to herself, to see and to hear and to understand clearly. While English translations have homogenized all the Marys, Marias, and Miriams into the singular "Mary," John's Greek is clearly "Mariam" a version of "Miriam." The name recalls that first Miriam, from the Book of Exodus, who arranges the rescue of her brother, the infant Moses, from being drowned by the Egyptians in the Nile, and who together with her brothers, Aaron and Moses, leads the people in the wilderness. While this is Mary Magdalene's last appearance in the New Testament—unlike the mother of Jesus, Luke does not mention Mary Magdalene in the Book of Acts; Paul never mentions her—perhaps like that earlier Miriam, she also led the followers of Jesus.

Indeed, perhaps like that earlier Miriam, she challenged the men for a leadership role. The first Miriam makes this challenge in Numbers 12:2, when she and Aaron ask, "Has the Lord spoken only through Moses? Has he not spoken through us also?" (Granted, things don't go well for Miriam here, but I do appreciate the effort.) Later Jewish tradition suggests that she had such a leadership role in the wilderness, and later church tradition suggests that Mary Magdalene also was a leader of the movement gathered in the name of Jesus.

Mary does not call Jesus by name; she exclaims *Rabbouni* (John 20:16), which John translates from the Aramaic as "teacher." John omits the possessive pronoun "my," which is part of the Aramaic word). Mary addresses Jesus not as "my lord" but "my teacher": in this identification, she intimates that she has more to learn, and so indirectly prepares for the descent of the Paraclete (see below), who will continue to teach the disciples after Jesus ascends to the heavens. Mary here associates herself with others who addressed Jesus with variations of this title.

First are the future disciples who in John 1:38 ask Jesus "Rabbi, where are you staying?" They will learn about those many mansions;

they will find him behind closed doors in a house in Jerusalem. Then comes Nathanael who, in 1:49, announces, "Rabbi, you are the Son of God. You are the king of Israel," the proclamation that anticipates Thomas's "My Lord and my God" in 20:28. In John 3:2, Nicodemus addresses Jesus with the title "Rabbi" and then announces that he must be a teacher from God, since no one else can do the signs that Jesus does. The reference to signs sends us to the other signs that Jesus will do as well as to the end of John 20, the chapter that presents Jesus's interactions with Mary Magdalene and Thomas; the Gospel proper ends with the notice that Jesus did many other signs, not recorded in the Gospel, but John records these to encourage belief (John 20:30-31). The other uses of "Rabbi" in the Gospel (3:26; 4:31; 6:25; 9:2; and 11:8) all give additional meaning to Mary's address.

Nole me tangere. (John 20:17)

In John 20:17, Jesus says to Miriam, "Do not hold me for I have not yet ascended to the Father." The verse comes into Latin as *nole me tangere*, "Don't touch me." I read the Greek as having Mary already touching, even clinging, holding on for dear life. She thought she had lost Jesus when he died; she does not want to lose him again. But she cannot keep clinging to his body. Both she and he have more to do.

I appreciate Jesus's explanation: "I have not yet ascended." Had he said something like, "I have to go on a mission trip" or "I have to speak to Peter and the Beloved Disciple," she could have clung to him all the way. She can go forward and backward; she can even stay in place. The one thing she cannot do is ascend to the heavens. The time for that is not yet. With this same line, Jesus also suggests both that his work is yet unfinished, as is hers.

Mary needs to release Jesus both so that he can ascend (the details of the Ascension appear only in Luke 24:51 and, in slightly greater detail, in Acts 1:9-11) and so that she can proclaim his resurrection to "my brothers" (since the masculine plural in Greek can include women, and since we know Jesus has women followers, the translation "brothers and sisters" is correct).

The words Jesus gives her to repeat to them are "I am ascending to my Father and your Father, and to my God and to your God" (John 20:17). The Christology in these few words is both profound and multilayered. First, Jesus here presents the relationship of the "brothers and sisters" to the Father as comparable to his own. They are all children of God.

Here is why the familial language of "brothers and sisters" is of import: not only are the disciples in one family, but they all can also regard both God as their father and Jesus as their brother. In this way, they are truly "born from above" or reborn into a new family. Second, Jesus has through the Gospel, starting in the first verse, both been God and been with God. Here he reinforces his subordinate status: the one God is his God too. Third, also throughout the Gospel, Jesus has insisted that God calls his own. Here Jesus is the first fruits (to use Paul's language from 1 Corinthians 15:20, 23) of the Resurrection: he is the bridge between heaven and earth. And again, we may think of Jacob's ladder, with the ladder replaced by the Son of Humanity in 1:51.

Finally, the concern for ascent is also a concern for descent. During the Last Supper discourses, Jesus tells his followers that he will send them another *paraclētos,* a term variously translated "advocate" or "comforter," even "defense attorney." According to John 14:26, this Paraclete is also the Holy Spirit; John 15:26 identifies the figure as the "Spirit of Truth." John 16:7 makes clear that Jesus must go away (that is, ascend), because if he does not, he cannot send the Paraclete to his followers. Later in John 20:22, Jesus breathes the Holy Spirit on his disciples. Acts 2 suggests that the Spirit descends on the Apostles at Pentecost, about fifty days later. Regarding this possible discrepancy (since the accounts need not be seen as mutually exclusive), the Spirit blows where it will.

I have seen the Lord. (John 20:18)

Mary's final words in the New Testament are "I have seen the Lord." John 20:18 continues by affirming that she reported to the disciples "these things he [Jesus] said to her." The disciples do not question her; neither do they acknowledge her. Like the Samaritan woman, she fades from the scene as the more recently evangelized take center stage.

Mary has discharged her immediate responsibility but not her long-term commission. To say, "I have seen the Lord" and then not to do anything about it would be a failure of vision and vocation. To be called by name by one's resurrected teacher—a name that not even the Beloved Disciple gets—is a call of personhood, of self, which can now be better known and acknowledged. As we turn from Mary to Thomas, who is with the disciples hiding behind closed doors, we can picture her as setting the better model. She was not afraid to venture out to the tomb, back to the house, back to the tomb, back to the house. Perhaps they will follow her model.

Or perhaps she and the other women disciples were in the house with the men, urging them to do more than cower. They may be urging still.

Doubting Thomas

Thomas is listed in the Synoptic Gospels (Matthew 10:3; Mark 3:18; Luke 6:15; cf. Acts 1:13) as among the Twelve; like most of them, he is indistinguishable from the rest. John adds more detail. First, John 11:16 and 20:24 tell us that Thomas, which means "twin" in Aramaic, was called "Didymus," which means "twin" in Greek. Other texts, such as the Gospel of Thomas, identify him as "Didymus Judas Thomas," which comes out to "the twin, Judas, the twin." From here we move to questions of whose twin: Is he the twin of Judas Iscariot, or of Jesus himself? This latter idea finds purchase in some Coptic texts, and it has precedent in Greek mythology. The name "Gemini" (yes, as in the Zodiac), comes from the myth of the twins Castor and Pollux, one a human and one a god; they are brothers to the sisters Helen of Troy and Clytemnestra.

For John's purposes, Thomas is a foil who, like Peter at the foot washing, misunderstands Jesus. Again, misunderstanding leads to understanding. In John 11:16, as part of the Lazarus story, Thomas says, perhaps sarcastically, "Let us even go" with Jesus to Bethany, "so that we might die with him." He recognizes the dangers that coming close to Jerusalem will bring. Jesus in this instance does not bother to respond.

In John 14:2, as part of the Last Supper discourses, Jesus tells the disciples that he must leave them, "to prepare a place for you." Thomas, functioning on the literal level like many of the people Jesus encounters, asks, "Lord, we do not know where you are going. How are we able know the way?" (14:5). He has missed the point. Jesus is on one level speaking about preparing a place in heaven. In verse 2, he mentioned that in his Father's house (on one level, the Jerusalem Temple; on another, heavenly abodes) there are many rooms (the King James Version's "many mansions" sounds more upscale) and that Jesus is going to prepare a place for his followers. But on another level, Jesus is not speaking just of a place or a route, he is speaking of his own body, person, model.

In response to Thomas, Jesus offers the famous comment in John 14:6, "I am the way and the truth and the life. No one comes to the Father except through me." Jesus was with God and was God. He is the one who prepares the way, and he is the way. He testifies to the truth and the life, and he is the truth and the life. The point is not either/or, but both/and; John holds together the earthly and the transcendent; the already and the not yet. Don't think too hard about these seeming paradoxes. Instead, let them wash over you (another Johannine metaphor), and work on you.

There is also likely an early church background to this discussion between Jesus and Thomas. The Gospel of Thomas, as mentioned above, and other so-called Gnostic texts, often promote the concept of secret or esoteric knowledge that, once the adept possesses, can lead to eternal life. Some of these texts denied that Jesus was fully human, incarnate, fleshy; some denied he died on the cross. Some denied the idea of a physical resurrection. The important concern was "knowledge" (Greek: *gnōsis*), not faith or trust or belief. Important was the individual not the community; important was personal information, not Jesus and not the cross. To Thomas's "show us the way"—which could mean "give us this special, secret teaching"—Jesus responds that one cannot get to that prepared place apart from the cross; eternal life or life abundant does not do away with physical death. Moreover, for John, salvation requires the cross.

Given this background, Thomas is the perfect figure in John 20 to express doubt about Jesus's physical resurrection.

When it was evening on that day, day one of the week. (lit. "of the sabbaths"; John 20:19a)

A lot can happen during the day. We started the chapter when it was still dark, and it is getting dark again. But now, this darkness has a special kind of light, since the disciples have started a new week, a new life, again, "day one." We do not know what they did between the time Mary Magdalene reported the news and the evening, but I suspect that they did not do much. The reason: John explains that "doors of the house where the disciples had met were closed on account of fear of the Jews" (John 20:19b).

I am not happy with this line. Not only does it suggest that the disciples themselves are not Jews (they did not suddenly during the day become either Greeks or Christians; the former term means "Gentiles" and the later would be anachronistic for John, since there is in the late first century no formal separation between Jewish believers in Jesus and other Jews), it also suggests that the news of the Resurrection did not embolden the followers. Mary Magdalene was not hiding, so why are they?

As we've noted, Jesus speaks of his "new commandment," that the disciples are to love one another as he loved them (13:34), which he then glosses, "This is my commandment, that should love one another just as I have loved you. No one has greater love than this, to give one's life on behalf of one's friends" (15:12-13; see also 10:11). Jesus is willing to die; the disciples cannot make their way out of doors? Mark 14:38 and Matthew 26:41 could be imported here: "On the one hand, the Spirit is willing; on the other, the flesh is weak."

Peace to you. (*John 20:19c*)

Suddenly Jesus appears. The resurrected body can eat, as we see in John's epilogue, but it can also walk through walls. Thomas had asked Jesus, "show us the way" and Jesus responded, "I am the way." Similarly shifting the meaning of words, John first speaks of closed doors, and then Jesus himself becomes the door, the way, the life. Back in that good shepherd discourse, Jesus had announced, "I am the door" (English translations usually offer "gate"; John 10:7, 9). Doors cannot keep him out; to the contrary, he is the door, the way, the path to salvation in John's Gospel. And now he has bypassed the door made of wood to show the way (the route, himself). Gates, doors, windows—they keep in, they keep out, and they can also represent the divine presence.

To what was likely the disciples' shock at seeing him, and probably also the great shame of being fearful, Jesus offers the simple greeting of "peace." The term in Hebrew, *shalom*, is both a greeting and a wish; it is an indication of friendship rather than enmity, of wholeness rather than brokenness.

John also notes that Jesus stood "among them"—literally, "in the middle." This incidental notice shows that he is in their midst, not by the door as they cower by the back wall, not in front of the lectern while they sit at their desks. He is amidst them, one of them, surrounded by them. He is once again their center. John reminds us of where we stand—whether at one's feet, or in the midst of the group; at the well or in the home, at a wedding or at a cross—all places that can be sacralized.

Following this greeting, Jesus displays to the frightened disciples his "hands and his side" (20:20). Flesh, again; bodies again; now hands, into which the nails were driven; his side, into which a soldier thrust a spear and from which flowed blood and water. His death was real. His body still bears the wounds of the cross. Jesus has overcome death, but he still bears its marks. Deaths, tortures, tragedies, horrific moments are not to be forgotten; to the contrary, they make us in part who we are. But they do not constrain us. We are more than the sum of our parts. Again, the present allows us to have greater understanding of the past.

The disciples, appropriately, "rejoiced when they saw the Lord" (20:20b). And Jesus repeats, "Peace to you" (20:21a). Thus, his first appearance to the disciples is bracketed by words of peace. Not words of condemnation or yet of command. Day one ends with the message of peace, and that wish should sustain the disciples in day two and four and four hundred.

As the Father has sent me, so I send you. (John 20:21b)

Now the commission, but one phrased in terms of continuity. While we know that Jesus must ascend for that other Paraclete to appear, Jesus's own presence is continued on earth not only by the Spirit but also by the disciples. We may hear echoes of the message to, and then by, Mary Magdalene: "My Father and your Father, my God and your God." As God the Father sent Jesus, so Jesus sends his own followers, with the goal that they will be as obedient to Jesus as he was to the Father. It's a difficult commission, but given relationship, continuity, and Spirit, not an impossible one.

Jesus breathed and says to them, "Receive the Holy Spirit." (John 20:22)

To seal this possibility, following this commission, Jesus "breathed" (we recollect that the words for "wind" and "breath" and "spirit" are the same in both Hebrew and Greek) and by this breath says to them, "Receive the Holy Spirit" (John 20:22). A single breath can convey the Spirit.

More, John offers a new creation, since Genesis 1:30, part of the creation narrative, speaks of all living creatures as having the "breath of life" and Genesis 2:7 states, "The Lord God formed the human being

(Hebrew *ha-adam*) from the dust of the ground (Hebrew *adamah*) and breathed into his nostrils the breath of life, and the human being became a living being." With his breath, Jesus recreates his disciples. They live anew.

A simple breath can convey the spirit. We can inhale and exhale and feel it. Take a deeper breath and fill our lungs with air, with wind, with spirit, with power. It's exhilarating.

If you forgive the sins… (John 20:23)

Even more, in what initially looks like a non sequitur, Jesus next announces, "If you forgive anyone's sins, they are forgiven to them; if you retain, they are retained" (20:23). Most translations spell out what seems to be implied: if you retain *their sins*, they are retained. This is a plausible reading. The community now has internal responsibility: forgiveness of sins is not given by an individual, but by the disciples. Given the allusion to Genesis, we may even see here the forgiveness of Adam and Eve (while the word *sin* does not occur in Genesis 3, the first man and woman nevertheless disobeyed a divine command) and of Cain in Genesis 4. The reset includes questions of sin and forgiveness.

There are other ways of understanding the verse. As noted, the second part of the clause does not speak of sins. Perhaps something or someone else may be retained. In Matthew 16:19, Jesus tells Peter, "I will give to you the keys of the kingdom of the heavens, and whatever you bind upon earth will be bound in the heavens, and whatever you loose upon earth will be loosed in the heavens." Matthew's verse can refer to sins, but given those keys, which suggest doors that open and close, the better reading would be people. Jesus repeats the point about binding and loosing in Matthew 18:18 in the context of membership in the assembly. And John's verse speaks just of retaining, not explicitly of sin. Thus, this verse in John could indicate that people in the community whose sins have been forgiven have been restored to the community and retained by it. We might recall from John here

Jesus's assertions that he knows his flock, will protect them, will not let them go, and will love them until the end (13:1).

It is in this complex setting of fear and praise, sin and forgiveness, peace and the Spirit, that we meet Thomas once again.

But Thomas, one of the Twelve, who was called Didymus [the twin], was not with them when Jesus came. (John 20:24)

Time has shifted. Jesus is no longer present, but Thomas—who was absent—now appears. We can expect Jesus to reappear, as he does in the Temple following the healing of the paralyzed man by the pool, and as he does following the healing of the man born blind. Here he leaves room for the Ten to testify to what they had experienced.

John 20:24 provides another example of presence in absence. We already know that Thomas is "one of the Twelve," so the notice signals that he is not where he should be. He reminds me of the lost sheep and the lost coin in the parables of Luke 15. His absence makes the whole incomplete. But it also speaks to more: Where was he while the disciples were behind closed doors? Was he cowering in an alley? Was he perhaps praying in the Temple, or sitting by an empty tomb? Did the other Ten (Judas having absented himself) wonder about his whereabouts? Did they send anyone to find him or were they too scared? Thomas's absence here reminds me, every time I read the text, to look around and determine who is missing: What student is absent from the zoom meeting (I send an email immediately) or the classroom (I contact the academic dean)? Who is missing from the family table? Who is missing from the congregation?

I also feel for Thomas here—the resurrected Jesus appears, and he missed it?

Finally, Thomas may not have been "with them"—just as Judas was not "with them"—because he may not have been of the same mind as them. The Ten remain disciples, and Thomas is outside. We do not know if he understood at all Jesus's comment about being the way; we do not know if he understood all too well the implications of his earlier comment concerning going to Bethany to die with Jesus.

Will he enter the light, or will he stay outside, where the sun is going down and it is getting progressively darker?

The other disciples were saying to him, "We have seen the Lord." (John 20:25)

The disciples repeat the words Mary Magdalene spoke to them, "I have seen the Lord" (John 20:18). Whenever anyone makes that claim, Mary's voice is echoed. The pronouncement leads to at least two other matters. First, now that one has "seen the Lord," what is one to do? Close one's eyes and attempt to revision the moment? Draw it? Proclaim it? Act on it?

Second, by what rationale do we accept someone's word for this claim? If a friend tells me that there is a person predicting the end of the world on West End Avenue in Nashville, I am inclined to believe the report. I have seen this fellow with his signs before, and I would not be surprised that he had returned. However, if this same friend reports to me that she has seen Jesus in the flesh at a baptism at Radnor Lake the previous Sunday, I'd be inclined to doubt, no matter how much I love her and trust her. I might go so far as to accept that she had a vision, and that she truly believed what she saw, so that I could acknowledge her truth. But would I believe in the content of her vision? I doubt it.

Unless I see in his hands the place of the nails and put my finger in the place of the nails and put my hand in his side, I will not believe. (John 20:25b)

I have some sympathy for Thomas, although Thomas, according to John, witnessed things that I did not see, whether feeding five thousand with limited resources or raising Lazarus from the dead. He should have been primed. I also recognize the historical aspects of his comments: to the followers of what might be called a Thomasine branch of the Jesus tradition, where there is no physical, bodily resurrection and where knowledge is more important than the cross, the line sets up the oppositional Christology.

The scene returns us to the Incarnation, the taking on of flesh, for it is flesh that is marked by the nails and the spear.

Then, a week goes by. A lot can happen in a week—I wish I knew what was going on in between the day Mary proclaimed the Resurrection to the disciples and Jesus visits them and now, "after eight days." The good news is that a week later, "his disciples were again in the house, and Thomas was with them" (20:26a). He has neither come to belief, nor has he given up on the possibility. He reminds me of Nicodemus: will he remain outside or come fully inside? Had Jesus appeared, following his death, to Nicodemus, Nicodemus would have become a disciple. On the other hand, Thomas joins the Ten behind the doors—they clearly opened to him—but Nicodemus does not.

Now the scene repeats. We are eight days later, which means another "day one"—another chance at a reset. The doors are again shut. But something has changed. Gradually, the fear is abating; gradually, the borders between inside and outside, heaven and earth, are dissolving. And again, Jesus "came and stood in the midst, and said, 'Peace to you'" (John 20:26b). Thomas now has the chance to do what the Ten did when Jesus appeared to them: he should have rejoiced. He does not. John thereby offers another variation on the scene.

Do not be unbelieving, but believe. (John 20:27)

Jesus, who evidently knew what Thomas had said to the Ten a week ago (had he been there, but no one could see him? Has he been there all along? Has he been *here* all along?), invites him to "Bring your finger here and see my hands; bring your hand and put it in my side." Thomas does neither. He does not need to do so to follow Jesus's command, "Do not be unbelieving, but believe" (20:27).

Thomas realizes that the body in which Jesus was tortured and in which he died is the same body that came through the shut doors and now stands "in the midst" that is, "among them." And he realizes that now he too is "among them," among the disciples, with Jesus in the center. The doubts are gone. And so he exclaims, "My Lord and my

God" (20:28). Echoing is John 1:1, the beginning, where the Word is with God and is God.

At the same time, we can zero in on Thomas, who speaks with very personal language, "*My* Lord...*My* God." Matthew 6:9 gives us "Our Father" and John gives us multiple examples of how Jesus's disciples are part of a larger family. But here, John gives us the personal. The resurrected Christ is not for Thomas an abstract concept or a creedal confession; he is someone personal whom Thomas can claim for himself while at the same time being able to share that personal experience with others. With appropriate attention to the titles "Lord" and "God" and the focus on Christology and theology, we can take the time to think of the personal. That personal experience, and recognition, is also part of the good news. Thomas may be a twin, but what he has here is entirely his own.

Blessed are those who have not seen. (John 20:29)

John recognizes the complications of time: the present informs the past; the hour has come and is and was. But time is also linear. Lazarus will die again. The disciples will die. John's appendix chapter, 21, tells us both that the Beloved Disciple has died and that Peter will die. Thus, to address this inexorable *chronos*, clock time, John ends the scene by relativizing the experiences shared by Mary Magdalene and the disciples including Thomas. While Jesus affirms that all who have seen his resurrected body are blessed, he also proclaims, "Blessed are those who have not seen and yet believe" (20:29). The term translated "believe" comes from the same Greek word that means "faith." Sometimes the story is enough.

EPILOGUE

Breakfast with Jesus

John's original text likely ended at 20:30-31, the notice that Jesus did many other signs that his disciples witnessed, but that John recorded the seven in this Gospel to promote and enhance belief in Jesus as the Messiah. Chapter 21, which begins with the uninspiring phrase, "After these things," recounts one more Resurrection appearance. The text looks like a repurposing of the story of the miraculous catch of fish from Luke 5:1-11. There, Luke's version of the call of the disciples, Simon Peter sees the huge haul of fish, falls by Jesus's knees, and exhorts him, "Go away from me, Lord, because I am a sinner" (Luke 5:8). Luke does not detail what kind of sins Peter committed; nor do we need to ask. In Luke's account, Jesus tells Peter not to fear, but that he and his associates will from now on be catching people.

According to Luke, Peter begins his discipleship with a confession of sin; in John's epilogue, Peter begins his own discipleship, apart from Jesus, with reconciliation. Thus, "After these things" means after Peter had denied Jesus but then had raced to the tomb, had experienced his Lord's presence behind the shut doors, and had received the Holy Spirit. He should be ready to go.

John 21:1 gives us another Resurrection appearance, now by the "Sea of Tiberias," otherwise known as the Sea of Galilee (e.g., Matthew 4:18), the Lake of Gennesaret (Luke 5:1), and a variety of other names. John had mentioned that the "Sea of Galilee" was also called the "Galilee of Tiberias" in 6:1, before the feeding of the five thousand, so we might expect lots of food. We shall not be disappointed.

More disconcerting to me is why Peter, together with the "sons of Zebedee" (John and James), Thomas, Nathanael "of Cana in Galilee," and two other disciples (John 21:2) are in Galilee by the seashore fishing for fish rather than people. The chapter begins with the impression that although the events are "after these [amazing] things," the men are back to business as usual. Indeed, in 21:3, Peter announces that he is going fishing, and the others join him in the boat. They fish all night, and they catch nothing.

One of those "two others" is the Beloved Disciple. We do not know who the other is...perhaps one of us?

"That night" (John 21:3)—the expression, given the past twenty chapters, suggests that the dawn is coming, the light is coming. Something is coming or, better, someone is coming. Like Mary at the tomb, it's a matter of time before, once again, everything changes. Right on cue, just after daybreak, Jesus appears on the beach, and right on cue, the disciples, like Mary Magdalene before them, did not realize that they were seeing Jesus (21:4). We have another variation on the theme of the dawn appearance, but matters seem to be going in reverse. Mary had not expected to see Jesus in John 20; she watched him die; she knew he was dead. But these disciples *have seen* Jesus, twice, and yet they still do not recognize him.

Jesus addresses them not by name but by the designation "Children" (Greek: *paidia*). He could have called them "brothers" but instead he recalls to them their identity: "To all who received him, who believed in his name, he gave power to become children (*tekna*) of God" (John 1:12). More, he has also told them, "While you have the light, believe in the light, so that you may become children (*huioi*) of light" (John 12:36). In 13:33, Jesus even calls them "Little children" (*teknia*). There are several different Greek terms for "children," but they amount to the same sense of caring for those who need care, waiting for maturity, love. The term "children" can be infantilizing; in John 21 it is both an indication that the disciples need a bit more maturing, and a signal that they are still part of Jesus's beloved family.

Jesus here takes the paternal role, which is appropriate for the one Thomas called "My Lord and my God."

Jesus advises the men to cast the nets overboard one more time, and the catch is enormous.

With this sign of the catch, the Beloved Disciple catches on. He says to Peter, "It is the Lord" (John 21:7a). What would we do under such circumstances? Reactions such as praising God, or asking questions (Where have you been? May I join you?), or awaiting a new commission come to mind. On the other hand, might we wonder if we had been caught doing something other than what we should be doing? In this new time, can anything be business as usual? Peter, instead of worshipping, puts some clothes over this naked body and jumps into the sea (21:7b). Most commentators suggest he is swimming toward shore; he may equally be attempting to escape Jesus. Does he fear being condemned for not doing enough? Does he fear that he will follow in Jesus's footsteps and die?

I find interesting the comment about Peter having put on clothes. Jesus would have been crucified nude; the soldiers cast lots for his garments. It is unlikely, however, that Mary Magdalene encountered a nude fellow in the garden. A gardener is one thing; a naked gardener is just wrong. (Somehow, Jesus in the garden obtained clothing; John had more important things to talk about.) Mark mentions a nude fellow fleeing from Gethsemane (Mark 14:51-52). But why mention, indirectly, Peter's nudity?

In one respect, we are always naked before the divine, for in traditional theology, there is nothing God does not know, or see. In another, that nudity reminds us of Eden, where we were naked and not ashamed (or for that matter disappointed). But nudity makes us feel exposed and so vulnerable. Peter had no problem being nude in front of his fellow disciples, but to be nude in front of Jesus he could not bear.

The other disciples come into the boat, drag it to the shore, and there they find Jesus, by a heap of hot embers (most translations offer "charcoal fire"), with fish on it, and bread (John 21:9). He appears to have prepared the meal. The only other time we find a mention of a "heap of hot embers" is in John 18:18, where not Jesus, but the enslaved people and the police had made a fire, where Peter comes to warm himself, and where he will deny Jesus three times. This breakfast becomes the redo.

Wanting the men to join, Jesus invites them to bring some of the fish they had just caught. Peter brings in the net with 153 fish. We noted in discussing the fellow who had been paralyzed for thirty-eight years, that St. Augustine explained the 153 as the sum of the first seventeen numbers (1+2+3...). Otherwise put, this was a lot of fish, just as at Cana there was a lot of wine and at the feeding of the five thousand there were twelve baskets of leftovers (John 6:13). The messianic age is a time of abundance, of food, of wine, of life. I do find amusing the idea that one of the disciples took the time to count the fish. John does give the impression of precision.

Jesus invites the men to join him for breakfast. In 21:12, John notes that none of them dared to say "Who are you" because they "knew it was the Lord." The line is a paradox: they do not need to ask, let alone dare, because they know who is inviting them to eat. At times, we know something, but we dare not ask if what we know is the case, because we do not want it confirmed. The best example I know of such cases is when we are aware that a loved one has died. We know for a fact that there is no life in the body, but we dare not ask, for the verbal confirmation makes things too real. Perhaps the men are ashamed that they are back to business as usual. Perhaps they feel that they have not done enough for the Lord who gave up his life for them.

Jesus does not come to provoke feelings of inadequacy. He takes the bread and gives it to them, and also the fish (21:13), just as he did at the feeding of the five thousand. It's all good. The following triple request for Peter to express his love for Jesus reverses the three denials, and the command to feed Jesus's sheep allows Peter to follow the role of his Lord. It's all good.

We leave the disciples on the beach, in the glow of the embers, with grilled fish and bread in their bellies, and rekindled fire in their hearts. They have returned to where they started, where they first met Jesus, and yet something is different. Many things are different. They feel the breeze coming up from the lake, smell the fish and the fire, taste the breakfast, hear the voice of Jesus. Their senses are all heightened; their world is brighter, their life more abundant, and harvest ready for them. Breakfast is over, the sun is getting higher in the sky—time (*kairos*) to move into the light.

Watch videos based on *The Gospel of John: A Beginner's Guide to the Way, the Truth, and the Life* with Amy-Jill Levine through Amplify Media.

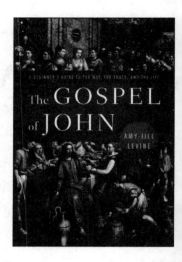

Amplify Media is a multimedia platform that delivers high-quality, searchable content with an emphasis on Wesleyan perspectives for churchwide, group, or individual use on any device at any time. In a world of sometimes overwhelming choices, Amplify gives church leaders and congregants media capabilities that are contemporary, relevant, effective and, most important, affordable and sustainable.

With *Amplify Media* church leaders can:

- Provide a reliable source of Christian content through a Wesleyan lens for teaching, training, and inspiration in a customizable library
- Deliver their own preaching and worship content in a way the congregation knows and appreciates
- Build the church's capacity to innovate with engaging content and accessible technology
- Equip the congregation to better understand the Bible and its application
- Deepen discipleship beyond the church walls

Ask your group leader or pastor about Amplify Media and sign up today at www.AmplifyMedia.com.